MW01006376

SPIRI
POWER
AND
MISSIONS

Evangelical Missiological Society Series
Number 3

Evangelical Missiological Society Series

#1
SCRIPTURE AND STRATEGY
The Use of the Bible in Postmodern Church and Mission
by David Hesselgrave

#2
CHRISTIANITY AND THE RELIGIONS
A Biblical Theology of World Religions
Edward Rommen and Harold Netland, Editors

#3
SPIRITUAL POWER AND MISSIONS
Raising the Issues
Edward Rommen, Editor

These books are available from the publisher:
William Carey Library
P.O. Box 40129
Pasadena, California 91104
800-647-7466

SPIRITUAL POWER AND MISSIONS
Raising the Issues

Edward Rommen, Editor

**Evangelical Missiological Society Series
Number 3**

William Carey Library

PASADENA, CALIFORNIA

Published by
William Carey Library
P. O. Box 40129
Pasadena, California 91114
(818) 798-0819

ISBN 0-87808-377-4

CONTENTS

INTRODUCTION

Edward Rommen

"Finally we are getting somewhere. We have rediscovered the tools we need to break through Satan's fortifications and press on to the final, victorious stage of world evangelization."

"I'm getting tired of this, every group that comes through wants to 'break down strongholds,' do a prayerwalk and guarantee our evangelistic success. Of course, no one seems willing to stick around, learn the language, learn the culture and do the hard work of communicating the Gospel."

Who should take credit for the fruits of the Romanian revolution? The itinerant prayer warriors from the West[1] or the faithful Christians who endured the many years of hardship under the communist dictatorship?[2]

These are just a few examples of issues that have surfaced in what has become a very intense discussion about spiritual power and missions. Twenty years ago the idea of spiritual warfare[3] did not generate any unusual interest. This is not to say there was nothing going on. Open confrontation with the powers of darkness has been a part of Christianity throughout its history. As a result there is a well established body of literature, including carefully formulated doctrines, and the reports of

---

[1] This is essentially what Eastman claims, when relating a story of prayer travelers who symbolically planted the "seeds" of the Romanian revolution (Eastman 1994:11-19).

[2] According to some accounts it was the courageous stance of one Hungarian Reformed Pastor, Laszlo Tokes, in the city of Timisoara which ignited the revolution (Tokes 1994).

[3] The term "spiritual warfare" has, of course, been used in many different ways. The range of meanings is illustrated by the fact that the term has been associated with the abundant life (Hall 1968), military strategy (Wilson 1964), as well as deliverance ministries (Warner 1991).

Councils. The ancient church used exorcists,[4] treated supernatural opposition as a reality, and faced it squarely. Power encounter was a regular feature of Medieval Missions.[5] Response to Satanic opposition played a significant role during the reformation.[6] Yet no "movement" developed.

Today things are quite different. Spiritual warfare, has riveted the attention of the evangelical community. Everyone seems to be talking about it. Indeed, there has been an explosion of books, seminars, conferences, and courses during the last decade. Debates rage. Tensions are on the rise. Accusations, counter accusations and even schism threaten not only the unity of the church but the missionary enterprise itself. So, where has this sudden intensification of interest come from? What could explain the rise of such concern at this time? Why today?

HISTORICAL CONTEXT

Referring to the current interest in spiritual warfare as a movement may imply a more well defined entity than actually exists. The interest grows out of such a wide range of Christian traditions and raises such a diverse catalog of issues as to almost defy being described by one concept. This broad-based initiative includes a wide range of individuals, organizations, and perspectives. By way of example, consider the variety of groups focusing on prayer, which is just one of many emphases in the movement: David Bryant and the Concerts of Prayer Movement; Peter Wagner and the AD2000 and Beyond Movement's prayer track; Cindy Jacobs and her Generals of Intercession, Dick Eastman and Every Home for Christ; Steve Hawthorn and Graham Kendrick with their emphasis on prayerwalking.

In spite of this diversity, it is relatively easy to sketch out the broad outlines of the movement's historical development.

---

[4] Eusebius quotes a letter sent by Bishop Cornelius to the Bishop of Antioch in 252. In it Cornelius says that the church of Rome had, among other officers, 52 exorcists (Eusebius VI 43,11)

[5] The accounts of Bishop Ansgar's activities on his mission to Scandinavia certainly fall into this category. These include: asking God to determine the outcome of a casting of lots and asking God to demonstrate His power over the weather (Robinson 1921:62-69).

[6] In a letter to the Wittenberg Theologians Dr. Johannes Bugenhagen Pomeranus describes a case of demon possession in the town of Lübeck in 1530 (Montgomery 1973:180-187).

There are at least four historical paths along which this "movement" has developed.

1. The General History of the Church. If we had nothing else, we could point to many examples of warfare prayer, power encounter, exorcisms, and healings throughout the history of the church (Wimber 1986:157-185). It seems that almost every generation of believers has had to face spiritual enemies of the faith. Surely there have been many denials and many failures. Nevertheless, there appears to be an unbroken chain of experience, which points to the persistent reality of the spiritual battle. This heritage ought to be examined carefully, for surely it will yield many lessons.

2. The History of Missions. More specifically, these phenomena have been part and parcel of the church's experience on the front-edge of its advance. Missionaries in their encounter with other religions and cultures have been forced to take spiritual opposition seriously. For example, Allan Tippett directed our attention to the need for what he called Power Encounter, which, in his opinion, was the only way to affect a secure and lasting conversion from animism to Christianity.[7] Although he may not have used this term in exactly the same way as many do today, Tippett's work illustrates one attempt to come to grips with the power-struggle so often encountered by missionaries.

3. The Concerns of Ministry Strategy. As the missionary enterprise unfolded, some of its creative energy was poured into the development of effective strategies. How can we most effectively fulfill the missionary mandate. A recent example of this concern can be seen in the Church Growth movement. Initially focused on the use of the social sciences as a means of affecting growth, some of its leading proponents began to emphasize spiritual means of growth. This is quite apparent, for example, in C. Peter Wagner's pilgrimage from Church Growth, to Signs and Wonders and on to Spiritual Warfare (Wagner 1987). A concern for strategy, then, eventually leads to asking (or re-asking) the

---

[7] Tippet describes the path from a pagan context to Christianity in terms of four major steps, each of which represents a process of some duration: a period of awareness, a period of decision, a period of incorporation, and a period of Maturity. After the second stage he envisions the need of a punctilliar encounter, a putting to an end the struggle for decision, which involves a putting to the test of the old powers. Once these powers have been shown to be inferior, regression becomes unlikely (Tippett 1977: 42-47).

questions of how our Spiritual Weapons can be used to effect growth.

4.   Recent Renewal Movements.   The emphasis on the miraculous has been a constant theme in many renewal movements, particularly in this century, including the classical Pentecostal renewals and the more recent charismatic renewals.   Interestingly, it seems as though many of these concerns converged with those of the Signs and Wonder Movement.

The modern spiritual warfare "movement" is the composite of ancient and modern concerns that have flowed together via at least four paths.   This general flow of history could be diagrammed as follows and shows that in one way or the other many of us have been, are or should be involved in the discussion.

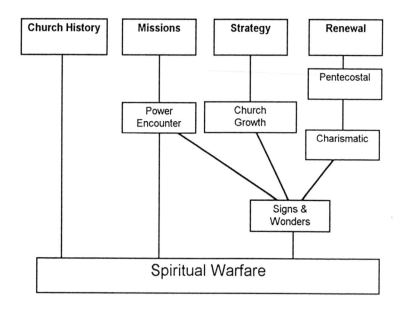

REASONS FOR RENEWED INTEREST

It is one thing to make general observations about the historical development of a movement.   It is quite another thing to attempt to explain why such an explosion of interest should have occurred now? Perhaps the survey of the movement's historical development itself points to factors which may have contributed to, sparked or even made possible such contemporary interest.

1. One reason might be that the prevailing world-view of the West has undergone profound change. The modern rationalistic, godless orientation appears to be crumbling. Many are no longer so sure that the supernatural and God can be denied. In fact, the bankruptcy of our social and intellectual programs have left us without answers and receptive to whatever might be out there. This openness is expressed, among other ways, in the renewed interest in the occult, Eastern mysticism, and New Age. These trends can be seen in films, literature, and even music.

Christians, of course, have not remained unaffected. One of the most telling changes in the church has been the effect which the reports of the experience of foreign missionaries are having. Coming from areas of the world in which the supernatural, the miraculous, and the mystical are accepted, missionaries do not hesitate to speak of demons, exorcisms, miracles. In the context of fading secularism, parishioners no longer view the reports as exotic curiosities, but as possible answers to their own questions. It seems that western Christians are no longer as willing as they once were to discount or even ridicule such reports.

2. Failure of many missionary strategies. In spite of the promise and potential of recently developed strategies, few pastors and missionaries have experienced the kind of success envisioned by the vendors of such growth schemes. How many pastors have been able to start from scratch and raise up megachurches? How many missionaries have been able to penetrate the bastions of resistant people groups?

When one set of tools or strategies proves inadequate, new ones are sought. Could it be that the frustration of disappointed pastors and missionaries is fueling the interest in these "new" techniques. If tearing down strongholds is presented as a guarantee for evangelistic success, its popularity is no mystery.

If the drive for success in ministry is driving the movement then it might be seen as a logical extension of pragmatism. So, if prayer walking appears to be a "cost effective" way of involving people in missions without requiring long term commitment it will be understandably attractive.

3. Is this demand for power a result of a sense of help-lessness?[8] Many appear to have come to the ends of their missio-strategic ropes. They are convinced that they have tried almost everything--to little or no avail. As a result they feel powerless and helpless.

This could, of course, set us up for dangerous abuse by the enemy. It would be a small thing for Satan and his opportunistic agents to capitalize on our fears and maneuver us into untenable positions. We could be manipulated and deceived into thinking, acting and planning in ways which run counter to the principles of the Gospel. We might even unwittingly import non-biblical material and syncretize the entire missionary enterprise.

On the other hand, a sense of powerlessness might well bring us to our knees. With the clarity of vision occasioned by humility and utter dependence on our Lord, we just might discover, that is re-discover, the very weapons we have neglected. After all St. Paul did tell us what the battle was about and what our armor should be -- and it wasn't a marketing strategy. Does our failure represent an opportunity?

So we ask, how does scripture define spiritual warfare? Is it an indispensable element of missionary advance? Does it simply represent a new and improved strategy? Is it an opportunistic manipulation of fears by those seeking to take advantage of the deep-seated discouragement and resignation of many practitioners? Or is it an opportunity to rediscover those spiritual weapons, which, in spite of our neglect, have always been the best way for us to advance the cause of Christ?

THIS BOOK

In order to move the discussion forward we have invited several authors, representing a wide range of positions, to address this topic. As the reader will note, they not only highlight the crucial issues, they also interact with one another. In doing so, they not only provide a wealth of information but model the type of substantive interaction we hope will characterize the ongoing discussion within the EMS.

---

[8] Power seeking as a response to powerlessness is one of the main theses presented in Power, Pathology, Paradox (Shuster 1987).

Chapter one is a revision of a paper read during the EMS annual meeting in November, 1994.   Authored by Robert J. Priest, Bradford A. Mullen and Thomas Campbell, it raises a number of concerns they have about current teaching on spiritual warfare. Originally it was to have been one of the chapters in EMS Vol. 2 on Christianity and the Religions. However, in light of the importance of spiritual power to missions and the need for open dialogue, it was decided to solicit responses and publish them in the present format.

Chapter two, written by Charles Kraft, is one such response. After reviewing the final draft of chapter one Kraft not only interacts with the issues raised by Priest, Mullen, and Campbell, he also provides an energetic defense of one perspective on spiritual power and missions. Throughout this chapter references to chapter one are marked with page numbers. This should facilitate active interaction by enabling the readers to evaluate for themselves Kraft's responses to chapter one.

Chapter three is also a response, but of a somewhat different nature. In it Patrick Johnstone seeks to point the way toward an effective continuation of our dialogue on the issues of spiritual power. He endeavors to point us beyond the debate itself and reminds us of the centrality and efficacy of prayer.

As the reader will observe, we have only initiated the discussion. Priest, Mullen, and Campbell have not had an opportunity to respond to Kraft or Johnstone. Likewise, Johnstone was not given a chance to respond to Kraft. Nevertheless, it is our hope that these papers will serve to initiate a substantive but irenic dialogue within the EMS. Should this occur, it will serve as preparation for next year's (1996) annual theme, "Mission and the Holy Spirit."

We want to face the issues squarely, avoid being sidetracked by inconsequential matters, and above all, advance the kingdom of God. We invite the readers to examine for themselves the issues raised by these authors and trust that this will servo not only as a discussion starter but as a small contribution towards refining our understanding of this topic.

REFERENCES CITED

Eastman, Dick
>1994   *The Jericho Hour*. Altamonte Springs: Creation House.

Eusebius. *Church History*.

Hall, Charles A. M.
>1968   *With the Spirit's Sword: The Drama of Spiritual Warfare in the Theology of John Calvin*. Richmond Va: John Knox Press.

Montgomery, John Warwick.
>1973   "A Reformation-Era Letter on Demon Possession" In *Principalities and Powers*. Minneapolis: Bethany Fellowship, 180-187.

Robinson, Charles
>1921   *Anskar: Apostle of the North*. Translated from Rimbert's *Vita Anskarii*, London: SPG.

Shuster, Marguritte
>1987   *Power, Pathology, Paradox*. Grand Rapids: Zondervan.

Tippett, Allan
>1977   *The Deep-Sea Canoe*. Pasadena: William Carey Library.

Tökes, Laszlo
>1991   *The Fall of Tyrants: The Incredible Story of one Pastor's Witness, the People of Romania, and the Overthrow of Ceausescu*. Wheaton: Crossway Books.

Wagner C. Peter
>1987   *Signs and Wonders Today*. Altamonte Springs: Creation House.

Warner, Timothy
>1991   *Spiritual Warfare*. Wheaton: Crossway Books.

Wilson, James I.
>1964   *Principles of War*. Annapolis, Md.: Christian Books in Annapolis.

Wimber, John
>1986   *Power Evangelism*. San Fransico: Harper and Row.

MISSIOLOGICAL SYNCRETISM: THE NEW ANIMISTIC PARADIGM

Robert J. Priest, Thomas Campbell, and Bradford A. Mullen[1]

INTRODUCTION

Jim and Pilak hit it off together right away. As they parted Pilak pulled out a doll and pressed Jim to accept the gift as a token of his friendship. But when Jim showed it to the missionary couple in whose home he was staying, they gasped with dismay. They informed him that things were different on the mission field, that here people were involved with demonism, sorcery, and witchcraft. They told stories of people who accepted gifts that had been cursed, gifts with demonic influences attached, gifts which transmitted demonic influence, harm and death. They called for immediate prayer to put a hedge of

---

[1] The leading author of this paper, Robert Priest, is an anthropologist. He grew up in the Bolivian Amazon where his parents were missionaries to the Siriono Indians. For his doctorate (at U.C., Berkeley) he conducted 20 months of fieldwork with another Amazonian tribe, focusing his research on Aguaruna traditional religion and conversion to Christianity. He is presently Associate Professor of Missions and Intercultural Studies at Columbia Biblical Seminary and Graduate School of Missions--a division of Columbia International University (CIU).

A former missionary, Thomas Campbell presently serves as business manager of Columbia International University (and adjunct philosophy professor at Columbia Bible College--a division of CIU). He brings a lay concern and perspective to the issues of this paper.

Bradford Mullen is Associate Professor of Theology at Columbia Biblical Seminary and Graduate School of Missions. His specialties in Biblical hermeneutics, sanctification, and apologetics are directly relevant to the issues addressed in this paper.

protection around him and his wife and baby, and told him he should destroy the doll immediately.

Around the world, adherents of non-Christian religions have been affected by their encounter with Christian missionaries. But it is equally true that missionaries have been affected by their encounter with adherents of other religions. Western missionaries come from societies in which witchcraft, sorcery, magic, omens, divination, spirits of the dead, and spirits of other kinds, are--or have been until recently--absent from the cultural discourses of everyday life. They go to societies in which the cultural discourses constantly appeal to such realities, and take them for granted as explanation of all kinds of events and phenomena. In the face of such an encounter, some missionaries dismiss all such indigenous beliefs as superstition. But other missionaries observe that indigenous beliefs which assume the pervasive presence and activity of spirits somehow sound biblical. And they are disturbed to think that, perhaps, their own cultural background has hindered them from recognizing the presence and activity of spirits. Out of this encounter, many missionaries have rightly come to realize the need for rethinking their poorly thought through understandings of demonic realities. In reassessing such understandings, many missionaries experience what some of them have referred to as a "paradigm shift"[2]--a radical reorientation of their understandings of spirit realities and a radical rethinking of ministry strategy in the light of these perceived realities.

Such paradigm shifts have occurred in the lives of many missionaries since the beginning of the modern missionary movement. Until recently this has occurred on an individual and somewhat *ad hoc* basis. What makes the current situation unprecedented is the extent to which new doctrinal understandings of demonic power--derived from paradigm-shift experiences--are being formulated, systematized, publicized, accredited, and institutionalized in mainstream evangelical and missionary institutions.[3]

---

[2] cf. Kraft 1989:82ff; Kraft 1992:13; Murphy 1992:x; Wagner 1988a:42ff; Wagner 1994:154ff.

[3] A majority of missions-focused seminarians in America now take courses in which such new understandings are being taught as the basis for cutting-edge, essential strategy for effective evangelism. The number of new books and articles by missiologists about spirits and spiritual warfare is voluminous. These understandings are being institutionalized in various ways. The Prayer Track of

The ideas being advocated grow directly out of missionary experience with contemporary religious phenomena, and
accounts of such phenomena. New understandings of spirit
realities are being constructed by missiologists based upon
contemporary religious experience and upon a re-examination of
Scripture through the lens of such experience. As they construct
their arguments for how we are to understand spirit realities,
they continually appeal to accounts of contemporary experience
from which we are to infer truths about spirit realities--truths
which cannot be derived from Scripture alone. If the paradigm
shift being advocated involved an unadulterated return to
biblical supernaturalism, we would applaud it. But we fear that
such is not the case.

The paradigm shift advocated by these theorists is ostensibly a return to biblical supernaturalism in opposition to the
pervasive influence of enlightenment rationalism and naturalism. But in fact, this account of things involves a partial cultural
misreading both of "the West" and of animistic cultures. The
claim that enlightenment rationalism shapes the world view of
most westerners distorts reality. It does not take into account
the pervasive influence today upon the West of mystical
romanticism, existentialism, and "new age" spiritualities.
Western Christians are in danger of being influenced by opposite
and equally unbiblical philosophies.

But these theorists also misread animism. Many of these
authors are overly impressed with the extent of continuity they
find between the biblical view of spirits and the views of spirits
found in folk religions around the world, and are insufficiently
attuned to the degree of discontinuity between the two.
Furthermore, they fail to recognize the extent to which ideas and
beliefs shape human experiences of spirit realities and the
interpretation of those experiences. That is, embedded in every
account of phenomena related to spirits are ideas and beliefs. To
accept the validity of an experience and to draw inferences from
it, is often to accept unwittingly animistic and magical beliefs
implicit in the experience itself. Indeed, we argue in this paper
that many missionaries and missiologists unwittingly have

the A.D. 2000 Movement, for example, is being organized directly upon the
assumptions of these new understandings of spirit realities--in this case the
assumption of territorial spirits and the need for spiritual mapping (Wagner
1993a:12).

internalized and are propagating animistic and magical notions of spirit power which are at odds with biblical teaching, using such notions as the basis for missiological method. That such missiologists come from societies which are currently embracing mysticism, animism, and alternative spiritualities, doubtless contributes to this uncritical acceptance of animistic assumptions by missiologists.   In avoiding the Scylla of syncretism with rationalistic naturalism, many fall into the Charybdis of syncretism with mysticism, animism and magic.

These are serious charges. They are made, however, in response to dramatic claims made repeatedly and publicly, claims which have serious implications for the future of the missionary enterprise. Nor are we the first to express concern. Paul Hiebert (1989:117ff, 1992:41ff), Scott Moreau (1995), and Millard Erickson (1993:168,171) have all suggested that some missiologists are promoting a pre-scientific and magical world-view rather than a biblical one.[4] In a "Statement on Spiritual Warfare," the Intercession Working Group of the Lausanne Committee for World Evangelization (1995:156) expressed concern that recent missiological teaching on spiritual warfare is in danger of leading us to "think and operate [based] on pagan world views." But while others have sounded a general warning about "magical," "pagan," or "animistic" influences in missiological writings on spiritual warfare, we will attempt to isolate several specific ideas being disseminated widely in current missiological literature, showing them to be grounded in animistic and magical assumptions, rather than in biblical ones. Consideration of these may serve as a way to examine the presuppositions and strategies of a new paradigmatic approach to missions. We hope that this paper will provide a corrective to what we believe are erroneous assumptions and practices advanced by some contemporary missiologists, and that it will

---

[4] (See also, Powlison 1995:25, 59; Gailey 1994:250; Page 1995:251; Breshears 1994:15; Greenlee 1994:513; Wakely 1995:152-162.) This charge may seem strange, coming from Hiebert, since it was his celebrated essay, "The Flaw of the Excluded Middle" (1982) which pointed out western missionaries' inability to address adequately spirit beliefs and phenomena--an essay often cited positively by authors whose views we critique here. But many of those who cite his essay draw inferences from it other than he intended, and fail to heed the prescient warning with which he ends his article: that as we attempt to rethink our approach to spirit beliefs and phenomena we must not let Christianity itself become "a new form of magic."

stimulate discussion concerning the foundations for a consistent and biblical paradigm for Christian life and ministry.

In this paper when we refer to "magic," or "magical thinking," we have in mind two principles of thought which undergird most magical practice. *Homeopathic magic* is based on the principle of similarity or imitation--that like produces like. For example, if you can harm a doll made in someone's image, you thereby harm the person the image is of. *Contagious magic* stresses the principle of contact or contiguity, that physical contact transfers the character or properties of one item to another. Magic designed to heal a barren woman, for example, might apply contact with a fertile hen egg, thereby attempting to transfer its fecundity to the woman. An extension of this principle is the idea that two items which come in contact with each other come to share a common essence linking them together. By acting on one such object one can affect the other. By taking a person's cast-off clothing and applying poison to it, one harms the former owner with whom the clothing is believed still to share a common essence. Magic employing these two principles of thought is commonly referred to as *sympathetic magic.*

"Animism" originally referred to belief in spirit beings, and was intended to characterize all religion, including Christianity. Animism, however, has come to be used as a synonym for tribal or folk religion as over against the major world religions. Missiologists, in using this term, have stressed that animists are concerned with the powers of spirits and the manipulation and control of such powers. While magic proper concerns the manipulation of impersonal forces, animism may be thought of as a form of religion which employs the principles of magical thought to interaction with personal spirits and deities. Thus, the principles of imitation and contiguity are assumed to explain the operation of spirit power and are employed towards the control of spirits and their powers. When central American folk-Catholics wear the cross as an amulet to ward off evil powers, for example, animistic assumptions about spirit power are operative.

In this paper, when we refer to magic and/or animism, we are calling attention to the assumptions underlying magic and animism about how it is that spirit power is operative: specifically that 1) the principle of contiguity/contagion and 2) the principle of similarity/imitation are the bases upon which such power is operative.

The fact that this paper focuses on the dangers of syncretism with animism and magic, rather than with naturalism,
should not be construed as an attempt to deemphasize the latter
danger. As supernaturalists, we are concerned that our critique
not be construed in any sense as an attack on supernaturalism
and on the importance of prayer and faith to missions, or as a
denial of the powerful Satanic forces arrayed against us. Rather,
our critique is intended as an effort to disentangle and refute
certain limited magical and animistic ideas which are being
mixed with, and subvert, biblical supernaturalism.

NEW MISSIOLOGICAL DOCTRINES ABOUT DEMONS

We begin by summarizing four new[5] missiological doctrines about spirit realities. After pointing briefly to some of the
practical implications of these ideas, we will concentrate at
length upon the epistemological underpinnings of these ideas,
showing them to be animistic and magical rather than biblical.
We conclude by pointing the way for future reflection on this
topic.

Doctrine # 1: Vulnerability to Demons through Contact with Physical Objects.

First is the notion that dangerous demonic influences are
transmitted through contact or contiguity with certain kinds of
physical objects. The presence of such objects, it is claimed,
brings vulnerability to demonic influence. Timothy Warner, for
example, suggests that persons "engaging in occult practices may
invite demons to empower an object, and in this way the demons
become associated with that object" (1991b:93). "Evil spirits," he
maintains (1994:30-31), "use such objects as a medium to come to
people" and oppress them. Warner gives various accounts of
missionaries or missionary children who were attacked by
demons as a result of inadvertently being in the presence of such
things as a ceremonial dagger (1994:31), a tree (1991b:94-95),
and a demonized hill-top (1991b:89-90).

---

[5] New, that is, to the discipline of missiology.

Charles Kraft says, "Artifacts dedicated to enemy gods (spirits) have demons in them. Tourists and military personnel often bring from overseas . . . images or implements used in pagan rituals or dedicated to gods or spirits" (1992:112-113). While Kraft tends to stress the dangers of objects picked up overseas (see for example 1992:198; 1989:162; 1994b:55), he also notes that America is changing and that one can "pick up demons" in many places with links to the occult or the new age. He tells us, for example, that "so many health food shops are infected that we would be well advised to claim God's protection whenever we enter one" (1992:44-45). Demons also become connected with objects because of a death or prior evil act associated with the object. Kraft illustrates:

> A demon I once cast out of a woman claimed the right to inhabit her because she lived in a house in which a previous owner had committed adultery. . . . I have dealt with other demons who seemed to have rights to homes through occult activity, a death that occurred in the home and, on one occasion, a claim to a church through adultery that had been committed in the church (Kraft 1994b:43; cf. 55-57).

A building, Kraft tells us, "may be inhabited by evil spirits. If so, go through it room by room and break any evil power by sending away the spirits and inviting the Holy Spirit to take over" (Kraft 1992:198). Animals may also be demonized purposely and given as pets to people one wishes "to infect." Kraft tells of casting a demon out of a cat, and tells of another woman "who suspected her baby parakeet to have a demon and tested the theory by commanding it to perform a trick it had never been taught. It complied immediately and a demon was later cast out of it" (1992:234).

C. Peter Wagner suggests that even tourist replicas of traditional religious objects may be demonized (1993c:62). He tells how his own house was infected by demons because of infected decorative objects he brought back from Bolivia (1988b:64-67, 1993c:62-64). He suggests that "demons can and do attach themselves to objects, to houses or other buildings, to animals and to people" (1990:76), and argues that "any discerning Christian who has spent time in an animistic culture has no question about this" (in Archer 1994:55-56). He suggests that Christians may need to exorcise demons from their homes, demons which they may have acquired through infected objects or simply by visiting a pagan temple where a demon might have attached itself to them (Wagner 1985:76).

Ed Murphy also supports this doctrine. He writes of charms and other

> physical objects associated with the spirit world. Because they were dedicated to the spirit world when they were made, evil spirits are often associated with them. . . . This includes paintings, "art" objects, sculptures, images, charms, fetishes, books, even some forms of extreme rock (Murphy 1992:447).

Kraft, Murphy, Wagner, and Warner are four of the more prominent missiologists to accredit this doctrine, but the idea has also been taught by many others.[6] It is an idea which is now, particularly in missions circles, widely accepted as true.

Doctrine # 2: Vulnerability to Demons Through the Curses of Others.

A second new teaching is the idea that one is particularly vulnerable to demonic power when one has been cursed. Just as objects can be the medium of demonic transmission, so also words can be the medium of transmission.

Kraft argues that "satanic power can . . . reside in . . . words [as well as] objects. Satan can empower curses and other uses of words" (1989:162). He elaborates, "Demons [can] enter through cursing. . . . The power of the curse may be increased through the use of a ritual. In addition, cursed . . . objects in a person's possession can provide enemy forces the opportunity to afflict the person, even if not demonized" (1992:75, 76). Furthermore, Kraft contends:

---

[6] Thomas White (1990:105-106); John Robb (1993:178-179; 1994:182-183), Dick Bernal (1991:80ff), and Neil Anderson (1990: 222-223), to name a few.

> demons seem to be able to "hook onto" curses that have been leveled at a person's forbears. A prominent Christian leader converted from a Jewish family once described for me the total newness that came into his life when he was delivered from a demon hooked onto the curse the Jewish people put on themselves at the time of Jesus's crucifixion. . . . We once worked with a woman whose ancestry included seven generations of handicapped women. After the curse was broken and the woman was freed of the demon, she gave birth to a healthy baby girl (1992:76).

Ed Murphy also argues that the curses of satanists or those involved in the occult are efficacious (1992:443-445). He tells of a missionary to Africa who became "strangely" sick and could not be helped by doctors. Eventually, he says, "God revealed . . . [that] a curse had been placed on her. When the curse was broken, her body was then able to function normally. She was healed" (1992:444). Murphy tells of satanists who fasted, prayed and cursed certain Christian leaders--leaders who subsequently fell into immorality and were removed from ministry. He argues that we must not be complacent about the implications of such curses, but must "learn how to mobilize believers to warfare prayer to break these demonic curses" (1992:445).

Timothy Warner also argues that curses carry occult power. He tells of a church building which was cursed and needed to have the curse lifted (Warner 1991b:78). He also reports that the children of a missionary family cursed by a witch doctor turned rebellious on their next furlough until the curse was identified and the demons enforcing the curse were dealt with (1991b:103-104). According to Warner, the missionaries went astray by not taking the curse seriously, assuming that as Christians they were impervious to such a curse.

Wagner also supports the notion that believers can come under demonic bondage as a result of "curses launched at believers by individuals or groups" (in Archer 1994:54). Cindy Jacobs (1993:86) gives similar warnings of the efficacy of curses as do many others (cf. Prince 1986, 1990, Bernal 1991, White 1990:119-121).

Doctrine # 3: Vulnerability to Demons Through Genealogical Transmission.

A third new doctrine is the notion that demons are transmitted through genealogical inheritance. This may be associated with a family curse, or may simply occur naturally. A child, for example, may acquire a demon from his parents, perhaps at the very point of conception.

Timothy Warner (1991b:106-109) suggests that ancestral sins or occult activities give demons special rights to attack the descendants. Kraft suggests that when parents or ancestors dedicate their offspring to a spirit or god, or when they seek spirit power to become pregnant, or simply are involved in any pagan ritual or act--such as consulting a fortune teller--the child will often be "demonized from the moment of their conception" (Kraft 1992:73). "One of the laws of the universe," he says, "is that demons can be inherited" (Kraft 1993:262). He suggests the existence of "generational or 'bloodline' spirits" which typically

> have gained entrance through the commitment of or curse put on an ancestor. Such generational spirits tend to cause similar . . . problems . . . from generation to generation. . . . We discovered that one woman's grandmother, her mother, and she herself had needed hysterectomies in almost the same year of their lives. Though this did not prove the existence of a generational spirit, it alerted us to look for one, and we found it (1992:74-75).

Kraft explains that when faced with such situations, he

> will often feel led to take authority over the father's bloodline and then the mother's to break the power of and cancel all curses, dedications, spells, emotional problems, diseases, and any other satanic influence that may have been introduced into the person's inheritance (1992:151).

Ed Murphy also argues for generational demonic trans-
ference (1992:437-438; 472-473). And since adoptive parents
seldom know the full ancestry of their adopted or foster children,
Murphy encourages such parents, as a matter of course, "to take
their adopted and foster children through deliverance"
(1992:438). Neil Anderson also feels that "Adopted children are
extremely vulnerable to demonic influence," and that they

> come to their adopted parents with spiritual
> problems even as infants. . . . If you are thinking
> of adopting a child, we recommend that you . . .
> be present at the time of birth. You should dedi-
> cate your adopted child to the Lord immediately
> to assume stewardship and negate demonic influ-
> ence (Anderson 1991: 205).

Similar ideas have been taught by many others.[7]

Doctrine # 4: Vulnerability to Demons Because of Geographical Location.

A fourth relatively recent doctrine is that of "territorial
spirits"--the idea that certain spirits, particularly high-ranking
spirits, are territorially based, exercising their power over
geographically delimited regions. To be within the boundaries of
such regions is to be particularly subject to demonic power.
Indeed, the presence of powerful territorial spirits accounts for
why the gospel is resisted so fiercely in certain areas. Missions
strategy, therefore, must focus on spiritual warfare designed to
remove such territorial spirits, or to "bind" their power.
     One account, which advocates of this position have told
and retold, involves the story of a missionary passing out tracts
in a town in which the main street ran along the border between
Brazil and Uruguay (Shibley 1989:73-4; Wagner 1988a:201-202;
Wagner 1988b:60-61; Wagner 1990:81; Warner 1991a:52-53;
Warner 1991b:136-7; Kraft 1994b:60-61). When pressed to

---

[7] Thomas White 1990:61-66,87,121-2,154,159-60, 1993:93, 1994:36, Francis and
Judith MacNutt 1988:58-60, Martin 1988:63, Dickason 1987:219-221, Bernal
1991:25, Bauman 1988:115-116, and Sears 1988:107-8, 110. For a slightly different
approach see Kenneth McAll's **Healing the Family Tree.**

accept tracts on the Uruguay side, people were resistant. But when the missionary crossed to the Brazil side of the street, people willingly accepted the tracts and showed marked interest. Indeed, some of the same people who rejected the tracts when on the Uruguay side were receptive on the Brazil side. It is inferred that a territorial spirit was powerfully operative in Uruguay, while the territorial spirit on the Brazil side had been "bound." Simply getting people to cross the street put them on terrain where they were more likely to be receptive to the gospel.

Timothy Warner was the first leading missiologist to promote the idea of territorial spirits (Warner 1986:98-99). He argues that Satan assigns "a demon or corps of demons to every geopolitical unit in the world" (1991b:135) and that we must confront the "demons associated with specific locations or geopolitical units" (1991b:134).

Kraft suggests that "Cosmic-level spirits seem to exert what might be referred to as a "force-field" influence over territories, buildings, and . . . nations," that "Satan is able to counter the force field activity of God," but that Satan's force fields may be nullified "through cosmic-level spiritual warfare, leading to impressive conversions and church growth statistics" (Kraft 1994b:58). "It is amazing," Kraft notes (1994c:27), "how freely the gospel can be shared when the place has been "cleaned out" of evil spirits beforehand by commanding them to leave in the name of Jesus Christ."

C. Peter Wagner has done as much as anyone to support this doctrine, both by pulling together edited volumes on the topic (Wagner, ed. 1991; Wagner, ed., 1993), and by writing on the topic himself (1988a:196-205; 1988b:58-63; 1989; 1990; 1991a; 1991b; 1993a; 1993b; 1993c). He too argues that "high ranking . . . evil spirits" are assigned to territories to "prevent God from being glorified in their territory" (1990:77), and to "veil the gospel" (1990:75) within their region. He concludes that "if we could learn how to break their control through the power of God, positions on the resistance-receptivity axis [of given people groups] could change virtually overnight" (1990:77). That is, if we can "map" these territorial spirits and defeat them in spiritual warfare, we will experience an enormous upsurge in evangelistic fruit (cf. Wagner 1988a:58; Caballeros 1994:125-127; Warner 1991b:140).

Wagner (1993a:14) identifies George Otis as the "top leader" in the field of mapping territorial spirits. He is co-

coordinator with Wagner of the A.D. 2000 Movement United Prayer Track and leads its most prominent unit, the Spiritual Mapping Division (Wagner 1993a:12-14)--a division committed to mapping "enemy deployments worldwide, including territorial spirits, primary demonic headquarters or strongholds" (Yamamori and Otis 1992), and to mobilizing prayer based on such understandings in order to "bind the strongman" (Otis 1991:93). Otis' book, **The Last of the Giants** (1991), gives a classic exposition of this approach. Many others have been strategic in supporting and propagating this doctrine as well.[8]

PRACTICAL IMPLICATIONS OF THESE DOCTRINES

Before subjecting such ideas to analysis, it is worth pointing out that the truth or falsity of these ideas has great practical import.

1. Practical Import for Social Relationships

First, these ideas have import for social relationships. Let us return to the encounter between Jim and Pilak, the benefactor of the suspect gift. A few days after Jim got rid of Pilak's gift, they met. Pilak asked how his wife liked the doll. He emphasized that the doll was valuable; its dress was tied to old cultural traditions. He asked when he could visit and discuss features of the doll and its dress. Jim, having discarded the gift, stuttered out an excuse postponing the visit. Then he desperately scoured city shops looking for an identical doll to purchase. He was lucky to find one, though he paid dearly. The substitution worked. But he had a close call in terms of harming an interpersonal relationship. We recall another seminary student, with similar understandings, tell of receiving a valuable gift from an international student, and comment matter-of-factly, "needless to say, as soon as I got home, I burned it." Missionaries go to peoples around the world where gift-giving

---

[8] John Dawson 1989:151-160; 1991a; 1991b; Cindy Jacobs 1991:100-103, 222-247; 1993; Harper 1984:86-87; Shibley 1989:71-75; Lawson 1991; Lea 1991; Linthicum 1991: 64-79; Silvoso 1991; Sterk 1991; White 1990:118; 1991; 1993:133-142; Caballeros 1993; Hummell 1993:195-197; Lorenzo 1993; and Sjöberg 1993.

and interpersonal reciprocity form the basis of relationship. Missionaries who fear the possible taint of demons attached to gifts--whether of pets, of dolls, or of meat--are hindered in their ability to enter fully into reciprocal relations with those to whom they go.

When potential foster or adoptive parents are taught that infants whose ancestry is unknown may well carry demons passed to them genealogically, this too has necessary implications for social relationships. When adoption carries with it fear of potential exposure to demonic ties, it should not surprise if many decide not to adopt. And for parents of adopted children, there is the propensity to see genealogical demonic ties as causes of behavior problems. And what of the suggestion that all foster or adopted children be routinely exorcised? Whether or not one accepts this doctrine does have practical import for how such children are viewed and treated and for how such children are encouraged to understand themselves and the problems they encounter.

2. Practical Import for Spiritual Security

Second, these ideas have import for spiritual well-being. If we believe that we are vulnerable to demons because of inadvertent contact with objects, places, curses, and people, then our sense of spiritual security is affected. Take the case of Jane and her husband Tom, who had been exposed to these doctrines. As poor seminary students they jumped at the chance to house-sit for their seminary professor who was on sabbatical. But when they moved in, they were shocked to discover various tribal artifacts decorating the home of their anthropology professor. Jane became increasingly concerned, one day momentarily thinking a reflection in a window was a demon. With permission they removed the objects and put them in the professor's basement office, directly below their bedroom. But when Jane unexpectedly became pregnant, she worried about the condition of her baby. Then she had a dream in which Satan appeared and told her that he was possessing her baby. She told her husband. He subsequently had a similar dream. The seminary professor arrived home just at this moment. After prayer and counseling the couple resolved their fears. But we suggest that it was their prior acceptance of certain of the doctrines we are examining which predisposed them/made them vulnerable to the terrifying experiences which they had. Such doctrines do affect our sense of spiritual security.

What all these doctrines have in common is the idea that our vulnerability to the power of demons is based on nonmoral and nonspiritual conditions--conditions of physical contiguity and symbolic association with words, objects, persons, and places. Thus, Wagner tells us that "even believers living in holiness" are vulnerable to curses (in Archer 1994:54). Warner tells stories of missionaries who assumed that they were secure from such things as curses, based on their Christian position, but who discovered to their detriment that such was not the case. Kraft stresses that while sometimes people are demonized through sin, this is "relatively rare" among Christians, and implies that such demonization occurs more often through such things as genealogical transmission, curses, or inadvertent contact with some object (1992:47ff). He describes people from whom he casts demons as godly and spirit-filled.[9] Kraft writes, "When people become demonized through . . . inheritance, it is totally unchristian to suggest it was their fault. *They were victims and, in accordance with some law of the universe, they became demonized"* (Kraft 1992:48, italics in the original).

Christians have traditionally read the Bible as emphasizing that we need to fear Satan's influence in the doctrinal, moral and spiritual arena--that we need to fear sin and deception. These authors, however, tell us that we need to fear Satan's ability to attack based on factors other than our doctrinal, spiritual or moral response--that is, based on conditions of physical contiguity and symbolic association with words, objects, persons, and places. And they claim that their principles are based on "some law of the universe." Whether this law is taught by the Bible or merely by magical and animistic thinking has enormous implications for the spiritual well-being of believers-- and especially of missionaries--and for the spiritual focus of their lives. Do we seek to live lives worthy of the God who called us, trusting that any merely physical contact we might have with objects whose precise moral and spiritual history we are ignorant

---

[9] He writes, for example, "We were able to free her from nineteen demons that evening and one more two days later in my office. And Claire, though already a committed, Spirit-filled and actively ministering Christian, moved into a freedom she had never known" (Kraft 1992:15).

of is a matter of indifference to our state of vulnerability to the demonic? Or do we believe that gifts, houses, plots of land, etc. have the potential of containing demons such that physical contiguity itself renders one vulnerable to them? Do we believe that the secret curses of others render us vulnerable to demons? If so, then we need to devote attention and energy to the effort of decoding such possible ties. This of course suggests that we need special sources of knowledge to do so. The constant possibility of failing to decode some such contact rendering one vulnerable to demons, naturally introduces a measure of spiritual insecurity. Such doctrines do have enormous implications for the Christian life.

3. Practical Import for Missionary Methodology

Third, these doctrines have practical import for mission-ary methodology--for how we direct our efforts and allocate our resources. If it is true, for example, that demons exercise their deceptive power territorially, and that they can be combatted territorially so as to open people of that territory to the gospel, then anyone with a concern for the advance of the gospel will indeed be interested in redirecting our efforts and resources in such a direction. If Wagner is correct in saying, "Anthropology sees culture *as it appears to be,* while spiritual mapping attempts to see culture *as it really is*" (Wagner 1993c:57, italics his), then why devote intellectual effort to the mere appearance of reality when you can devote your efforts to reality *as it really is*? Recently a D.Min student proposed a thesis to one of us in which he would map the territorial spirits in a certain part of the world. He wanted to use this to lead groups of monolingual, monocul-tural Americans to the region to do prayer walks, and bind the territorial spirits, thus providing the breakthrough for the advance of the gospel [quite similar to the prayer walk described in a recent MARC Newsletter (March 1994, p. 1]. If such research generates true knowledge of unseen spirits, then many would be attracted rightfully to the pursuit of such knowledge and methods based thereon. But if untrue, those who embrace and propagate the tantalizing falsehood would divert valuable energies and resources from productive reality-based under-standings and methods. What missionary candidate would not love to find some key or shortcut obviating the need for laboriously acquiring linguistic and cultural competence--something missions is dangerously in short supply of?

EPISTEMOLOGICAL UNDERPINNINGS OF THESE DOCTRINES

Our concern about the new doctrines we are examining extends beyond their practical import for social relationships, spiritual security and missionary methodology. They also have enormous epistemological import. The doctrines we have presented are theories about spiritual realities not given in Scripture, something freely acknowledged by key proponents of these doctrines. Fidelity to Scripture requires us to "test" new ideas. When we question some accounts of the supernatural given by Kraft, Warner, Wagner, or Otis, we do so not with the commitments of enlightenment rationalists who refuse to accept the validity of any account of the supernatural, but as biblicists who refuse uncritically to trust reported experiences of the supernatural which advance "new doctrine." We do not cast doubt on contemporary accounts of the supernatural which are congruent with what we know about the supernatural from Scripture (as in many accounts of demonic possession). We believe in the supernatural--within the framework of biblical teaching. It is only when such accounts imply ideas about demonic power not given in Scripture--not demonstrable through careful biblical exegesis--and when such accounts are being appealed to as the basis for constructing new doctrine, that we are interested in submitting such accounts and doctrines to careful scrutiny. When the spokespersons for these new doctrines propagate those doctrines in public, and demand their acceptance on account of the reported experiences, then we have a solemn responsibility to subject such ideas and reported experiences to careful scrutiny.

It is fairly easy to determine the epistemological principles which the various authors propagating these new doctrines use to construct and defend them. In this section we pinpoint and critique these basic epistemological principles.

1. Interviewing Demons

As one reads these writings carefully, one is startled by the amount of information which is acquired by interviewing the demons in demonized persons.[10]   Thus Murphy gives great detail about a missionary wife whose demonization, it was discovered, was genealogical in nature.   He tells us, among other things, which demons entered her in the womb, which entered when she was sexually abused as a three year old and which entered her as a result of working with a pastor who was demonized.   A careful reading of the text makes clear that Murphy's source of information (given his own interpretive framework for the phenomena) was demons.   Later, when the woman watched a television show about "Satanic Ritual Abuse" and began to have "flashbacks" of her father abusing her in the same way, "The demons confirmed her flashbacks at every point" (1992:474). Again and again Murphy supports his notions through stories of demons who confirm the truths being propounded.   He claims, "I have learned how to keep demons from lying to me" (1992:53). He often commences an account with statements such as, "I forced him [the demon] to expose the entire demonic hierarchy working in the woman and in her entire family" (1992:53). Murphy justifies the truth of one extra-biblical concept by reference to an occasion when a demon explained the concept to him.   He concludes, "As I dealt with him, I found no reason for disbelieving his story" (1992:315).   After telling us various ways that people can "pick up" demons, he ends his assertions with the addendum, "as demons themselves confess" (1992:461).   And, indeed, on many occasions that is the only evidence he offers us of the truth of his pronouncements.   Many of his ideas about spirits, therefore, are derived directly from what, within his own frame of reference, demons told him under questioning.   Thus he

---

[10] We should point out that these authors take for granted that they are actually conversing with demons.   It may be possible that much of what they observe should be understood as something other than demon possession and demonic manifestations.   It is beyond the scope of this paper to explore such issues or possibilities. (For a thoughtful book which suggests that much which passes for demon possession is not, see Powlison, 1995.)   Although we lack sufficient knowledge and evidence to take a clear position on this, we simply note that the authors firmly believe they are talking with demons, and that biblical teaching does not preclude such a possibility.

develops his doctrine of the genenealogical transmission of demons, offering us little but the demons' own claims. He writes, "In several cases where severe demonization has existed since infancy, demons have declared their presence in the family line, sometimes for hundreds of years. There is no reason to doubt their claims" (1992:438). While he acknowledges that demons sometimes lie, he is confident that he can "compel them to speak the truth" (1992:30-31).

The method of Charles Kraft is similar. In **Defeating Dark Angels,** Kraft teaches that Christians are commonly demonized. He estimates that in many churches a third of the church members are demonized (28). He offers long lists of the "function names" of demons--including such demons as the demon of death, darkness, self-rejection, nervousness, rape, religiosity, lesbianism, compulsiveness, bulimia, caffeine and water witching (123-125). He discusses the language abilities of demons (56-59). He explains that demons which are found near bodily orifices (e.g., mouth, nose, eyes, ears, anus, or vagina) may be best commanded to leave through that orifice (194), as well as detailing other means of exorcising demons.[11]   Interspersed through it all are accounts of what demons told him.   Indeed, Kraft seems purposefully hesitant to cast out the demons, first engaging in extensive counseling in which demons are periodically called up to give more strategic information.   Kraft suspected that Donna, a demonized woman with a traumatic childhood, had a problem with her mother. She initially denied it, but "demons were contacted and the information we gathered," says Kraft, confirmed his belief that Donna needed to

---

[11] Kraft writes, "Anointing oil that has been blessed may help. I've found that some demons show no response to the use of oil while others seem to be freaked out by it. It is worth experimenting with. But don't use oil until you have empowered it by invoking Jesus's name over it in blessing" (1992:198). Later, he continues, "I have found the following effective with some demons but not with others: anointing oil (empowered by God through blessing it), eye contact, touching the person, inviting angels to torment the demons, making the sign of the cross, speaking in tongues, having the person drink water that has been blessed, forcing the demons first to see Jesus and then to face and look at him, speaking light into dark places where demons live, and threatening to send them to Satan or into the abyss. In addition, some deliverance ministers find it helpful to baptize the person, serve the Lord's supper to the person, and use blessed salt giving a few grains to the person every hour. I have found no method that consistently works well" (Kraft 1992:231).

address this issue. When counseling a demonized person with deep problems--such as five-year-old Ollie--Kraft suggests:

> it is helpful to call up a demon to get information from him concerning what to tackle next in the process of getting the person healed. . . . By using additional insights *revealed to us by . . . demons*, we were able to deal with a number of other events Ollie had forgotten about. . . . This is a typical way in which we discover, come in contact with, and then use the demons to help us deal with deep-level issues. . . . Frequently, by pumping them [demons] for more information . . . we can learn more about the kinds of things that need to be dealt with through inner healing. . . . When we're finished getting information from them, we send them to the feet of Jesus and ask Jesus to dispose of them (Kraft 1993:268-269, 270, 271-272; italics added).

Kraft has a fairly lengthy chapter entitled "Getting Information From Demons" (1992:157-175). In telling us how to do this, he suggests, among other things, that if a demon hesitates to give requested information because it fears retaliation by stronger demons, one may speak "a hedge of protection around the lesser demon to protect it from revenge" (Kraft 1992:203). Under such a witness protection program the demon will then "be able to supply the information needed" (Kraft 1992:204). Kraft, with Murphy, acknowledges that demons do lie, but feels that with spiritual authority and discernment it is possible to acquire new knowledge through questioning demons. Though Kraft also claims to get "words of knowledge" (i.e., personal revelation from the God of truth), he acknowledges that he learns more by questioning demons (i.e., revelation from the father of lies) than through words of knowledge (Kraft 1992:165-66).

In his quest for a basis for spiritual mapping, Wagner also entertains the possibility of acquiring information by interviewing demons. He tells of an exorcism by Costa Rican psychologist Rita Cabezas de Krumm of a demon named Asmodeo. The "demon identified himself as one of six princes that serve just under Satan, whom they regard as king." The other princes, Cabezas learned, are "Damian, Beelzebub, Nosferasteus, Arios and Menguelesh" (1988a:203). Wagner continues:

> Under each . . . are six governors over each nation. For example, those over Costa Rica are Shiebo, Quiebo, Ameneo, Mephistopheles, Nostradamus and Azazel. Those over the U.S.A. are Ralphes, Anoritho, Manchester, Apolion, Deviltook and one who is unnamed. Each of these governors has been delegated certain areas of evil. For example, the list under Anoritho includes abuse, adultery, drunkenness, fornication, gluttony, greed, homosexuality, lesbianism, lust, prostitution, seduction, sex and vice (1990:84-5).

Wagner's reaction to these "revelations" is curious. He grants that this is only "research in process" (1990:85), that "since demons are liars, one does not know exactly how much credence to give to such information" (1988a:203). He suggests, however, that mythology and apocryphal writings give evidence supportive of these claimed identities (1990:85), concluding that this provides "the most extensive clues I have yet seen to the identity of the top-ranked spirits" (1988a:202), and that this type of investigation is thus "worth . . . continuing" (1988a:203). A few pages earlier Wagner clearly implied that at least some exorcists can be relied on to know "exactly when they [demons] were lying" (1988a:183). He points approvingly to a list of named spirits which a missionary to Zaire cast out of a man as a further sample of what can be done to research demonic spirits and their names.[12]

While some who specialize in spiritual warfare (such as Neil Anderson) would not trust or seek to elicit "information" from demons, the authors cited above propagate ideas about unseen spiritual realities which were learned in large part by interviewing demons--by receiving revelations from those whose very nature and every action are characterized, according to Scripture, by deception and lies.

---

[12] "Guard of the Ancestors, Spirit of Travel, Feeder of the Dead, Rescuer from Sorcery, Voice of the Dead, Spreader of Illness, Paralyzer, Destroyer in Water," etc. (1988a:203).

God is a God of truth. We may trust His revelation. It gives us accurate knowledge of unseen spiritual realities. Because He reveals Himself, we can know about God what our senses and reason could not tell us apart from His revelation. This God of truth also reveals things about unseen demonic spirits which are not part of the physical material world--knowledge which is again beyond our capacity to acquire on our own. But what these authors suggest is that there is another source of revelation which we may access--the revelation of demons. While they claim that it is God's power which allows them to force the father of lies to tell the truth, the fact remains that the source of the revelation is demonic. It is not God speaking, but Satan. And the Bible tells us that ideas from Satan should not be trusted.

That Jesus, on a single occasion, asked a demon to speak and give its name (Mark 5:9; Luke 8:30) should not be used to justify the practice of interrogating demons in order to discover new truth about demons. The commentaries suggest various possible explanations of Christ's purpose in asking the demon to announce its name.[13] But whatever Christ's purpose, it was not to acquire needed information he could not otherwise know. This is the only occasion on which Jesus does elicit a response from demons. On all other occasions demons are silenced rather than encouraged to speak. Clearly Jesus is not intending to establish a pattern for His followers to practice of interrogating demons in order to acquire new information about the spirit world. If interviews with demons are such a rich source for acquiring new information about unseen demonic realities, why is the Church never pointed in this direction? Rather, we are told concerning Satan, that "there is no truth in him" (Jn 8:44). God warns His

---

[13] Given the widespread belief in antiquity (and in animistic cultures today) that one gains power over a person or thing by knowing its name, i.e. the name has an inner link to its object such that one can act on the name and affect the object, some scholars have interpretted Jesus' question as an attempt to gain control over the demon by knowing its name. Yet Jesus does not employ the name in this exorcism or ask for demonic names on any other occasion. Page (1995:170), who reviews the various interpretations of this passage, including the one just mentioned, writes, "Others suggest that Jesus asked about the identity of the demon in order to help the demoniac confront his own selfhood. Although this suggestion is probably closer to the truth than the former, it smacks of modern psychologizing. It is probably best to see the request for the demon's name as a means of emphasizing the severity of the demoniac's condition, for this is not just an ordinary case of possession."

people not to listen to those who are in touch with demons (Isaiah 8:19), and to have nothing to do with "doctrines of demons" (I Timothy 4:1)--doctrines, that is, whose source is demonic.

There would appear to be a very literal sense in which Kraft, Murphy and Wagner are propagating "doctrines of demons"--doctrines which they learn from demons. When Murphy, for example, asks a demon how it entered a woman and is told that it entered her at conception--passed down as a family demon--and Murphy then propagates the doctrine of the genealogical transmission of demons, it would seem that he is propagating a doctrine advanced by a demon. His assertion that "there is no reason to doubt their claim" is a denial of the biblical truth that there is every reason to doubt any claim made by Satan and his cohorts. Just as God is characterized by truth, so Satan is characterized by deception and lies. Unless we know on independent grounds (for example from Scripture) that what demons are asserting is in fact true, then we must not believe them. And when they assert something to be true which we already know to be true, their assertion of it should not add one iota to our certainty of its truth. Its truth must rest completely on other grounds.

It is worth reminding ourselves that what we are challenging here is the use of demonic utterances by leading evangelicals to infer and publicly propagate doctrines which cannot be inferred from Scripture alone, doctrines to which they are asking others to give mental assent. It is a serious epistemological flaw to develop and defend doctrines which stem from the "revelation" of demons.

2. Getting Information About Demons From Practitioners of Other Religions

The authors we are discussing assume that the beliefs about spirit realities held by practitioners of occult and animistic/folk religions correspond to reality. With some authors this is more implicit than explicit. Warner, for example (1991b:94), tells of a missionary who was warned by a local Filipino pastor that a spirit "was known" to live in the tree in his front yard. Warner implies that the missionary should have accepted this as true and should have acted on it. That is, the missionary should have accepted as true the local belief that this tree had a spirit. Warner also tells of other missionaries who rejected, to their own harm, the native assessment that a certain hilltop was demonic (1991b:89-90). The implication is clear--such a native claim about spirit realities should have been accepted at face value as true.

If one refers to what a group of people "believe," one's use of the term "belief" brackets out the question of whether such beliefs correspond to reality. But again and again we find these authors choosing to describe what people believe with words which imply that the belief really is true--words like "know," "understand," "recognize," and "perceive." For example, Dawson's comment (1991a:xvi), "Ancient peoples *were profoundly aware* of territorial spirits," is a typical instance of the pattern. Wagner suggests that among "animistic people the names of these spirit owners of territories *are well known*" (Wagner 1990:85-86). He writes, "Anthropologists and missiologists who live among certain people groups of the world today discover that principalities and powers are currently *known by name*" (Wagner 1992:147). The Tzotzil, Wagner informs us, "*know the names* of evil spirits who are assigned to various kinds of evil activities. They *know*, for example, that *Yajval Balamil* controls sickness, *Poslom* attacks people with swelling at night, and *J'ic'aletic* are looters and rapists" (1992:100-101). Otis tells us that in many non-western contexts "incorporeal beings *are perceived* to rule over homes, villages, cities, valleys, provinces and nations, and *they exercise extraordinary power* over the behavior of local peoples" (Otis 1994:35). Furthermore, these authors describe "cultural realities" in such a way as to imply that they correspond to actual realities. Thus, Otis (1991:91) writes, "One of the primary haunts of Haitian spirits, or *loa*, are waterfalls." Is this a statement about Haitian religious belief, or about spirits? In fact, to Otis, it is about both. For Otis, a single descriptive statement is sufficient because he assumes a correspondence between the belief and the reality.

In his quest to map spirits, Wagner tells us about a Nigerian, Friday Thomas Ajah. Before his conversion Ajah

> was a high ranking occult leader. . . . Ajah reports that Satan had assigned him control of 12 spirits and that each spirit controlled 600 demons for a total of 7,212. He says, "I was in touch with

all the spirits controlling each town in Nigeria, and I had a shrine in all the major cities." If this report is true, it would not be unreasonable to postulate that other such individuals, not yet saved, could be found in considerable numbers around the world (1990:76).

Clearly, Wagner is holding out the possibility that such practitioners of the occult could give us accurate knowledge about unseen spirit realities. He repeatedly suggests that native deities do bear a one-to-one correspondence with actual spirits, that animistic peoples really do "know" the names of the spirits. Thus he refers to *Amaterasu Omikami*, the Japanese sun-goddess, as the "territorial spirit ruling Japan" (1993a:53). Numerous articles in his edited volumes follow up his idea that native deities correspond to territorial spirits. Among these, Dawson writes (1991a:xv), "People are again openly worshipping the old territorial spirits. An example would be the renewed worship of Thor and Odin in Scandinavia and the reemergence of the druids in Britain." In the same volume Sterk (1991) offers an extensive treatment of territorial spirits among the Tzotzil of Mexico. He accepts the assumption that "The Tzotzils . . . are very aware of the names of many of the territorial spirits that inhabit their tribal area and villages" (159). He treats all of their beliefs about where spirits reside (in particular houses, underground streams, mountain peaks, caves, etc.) and how they exercise their power, as actual fact. What he is actually mapping is native belief about spirits. He assumes, however, that the belief equals knowledge, and thus claims to be mapping the spirits themselves. Chiundiza (1991) develops the idea that the traditional deities of the Shona are territorial spirits whose names and characteristics are known. Thomas White argues that demonic powers "coincide with the pagan gods and goddesses worshiped by the Greeks and Romans" (White 1991:61). Wagner suggests that the Old Testament pagan gods (Nergal, Bel, Merodach, Succoth Benoth, etc.) are the names of territorial spirits (1990:79-80, 85), as are the Greek and Roman pagan gods (Jupiter, Aphrodites, Diana, Poseiden, Bacchus, and Venus). It is quite clear from Wagner's following remark that he assumes that the names of pagan gods accurately correspond to evil territorial spirits:

> Research has turned up what is regarded by ar-
> chaeologists as the first known map of a city, the
> city of Nippur, the ancient cultural center of
> Sumer. . . . The features on the map, drawn
> around 1500 B.C., constitute what we today
> would call spiritual mapping. In the center of the
> city is written "the place of *Enlil.*" It is said that
> in the city "dwelt the air god, *Enlil,* the leading
> deity of the Sumerian pantheon." We would
> identify it as the territorial spirit over Sumer
> (Wagner 1993a:20).

Do cultural beliefs about the realm of spirits correspond
truthfully to actual spirit realities? The basis for such a claim
seems to be rooted in the assumption that just as God reveals
Himself truthfully, so Satan and his cohort reveal themselves
truthfully. Thus, Satan is assumed to give true information to
his followers, such as Friday Thomas Ajah. This is a rather
strange assumption to make, given what the Bible tells us about
Satan. There is no reason to believe that Satan has any interest
in being correctly known or perceived. Even if Friday Thomas
Ajah or Mike Warnke were involved in Satanism, the biblical
truth that Satan clothes all that he does in deception and lies
should be sufficient to inform and warn us that such spokespersons with close ties to the occult cannot be granted any authority
to give us new information about demonic realities. Their long
exposure and relationship to the master deceiver himself makes
them less trustworthy sources of knowledge about spirit realities,
not more trustworthy.

Not only does the Bible consistently stress that Satan is
characterized by deception and lies, it also consistently denies
that human religious ideas about deities and spirit powers
correspond to reality. The narrative of Scripture presents both
God and Satan as ontologically real beings who are actors in the
real world. It never presents Baal, Nergal, Succoth Benoth or
Diana as ontologically real beings intervening in the affairs of
humankind. Indeed Scripture warns us not to confuse human
religious phenomenology (human religious beliefs, practices and
artifacts--such as idols) with ontology. The emphasis of Scripture when discussing idols, or the worship of Baal or Asherah, is
a flat denial of the culturally postulated realities. The belief that
through the construction of idols, and the worship of spirits

associated with the idols, one taps into supernatural power is directly contradicted and mocked by numerous passages (cf Dt 4:28; I Ki 18:27; Ps 115:4-8; Is 37:18-19; Is 44:14-20; Is 45:20; Is 46:1-2,6-7; Jer 16:19-20; I Cor 8:4).[14]

On the other hand, two passages (Deut 32:17 and I Cor 10:20) indicate that when people sacrifice to idols, they are in fact sacrificing to demons. Does this idea contradict the more commonly articulated biblical assertion that idols are "nothings"? A careful look at I Corinthians 8-10 shows how the two principles are held in tension. Paul first asserts that idols and false gods are nothings (8:4). Then, he qualifies this by speaking of "so-called gods" which do have a certain reality (8:5). His use of the expression, "so-called gods," and his point that weaker brothers have beliefs about these realities which do not correspond to knowledge (truth) but which they have acquired by socialization in a pagan animistic context (8:8), points to the fact that in the minds of the weaker brothers such things were real. And what people define as real, has real consequences. Therefore, that reality--the culturally postulated reality--needs to be understood and addressed pastorally with sensitivity and respect, even though the actual ideas about idols, meat, and spirits do not in fact correspond to true reality. Demons do exist, of course. However, there is no simple congruence between what pagans believe about supernatural powers and what is actually true about demons. While pagan people's ideas about idols, spirits and gods do not correspond to truth, their involvement in a religious act of worship does constitute communion with demons. Paul denies that folk beliefs about such matters as idols, meat, or spirits accurately portray the nature of spirit realities, but does agree that spirits exist and are active in the systems of worship opposed to God.

Epistemologically, it is inconsistent and unbiblical to assume that folk beliefs about spirits bear an intrinsic truthful correspondence to actual spirit realities. If we proceed on the mistaken assumption that we can infer truth about spirits from people's beliefs about spirits, we will invariably end up syncretistically incorporating animistic and magical notions of spirit power into our doctrinal understandings of the demonic world.

---

[14] For a more detailed critique of this tendency to confuse pagan religious phenomenology with ontology, see Greenlee's (1994) excellent article on territorial spirits.

This is in fact what Kraft, Murphy, Otis, Wagner, Warner and others seem to be doing.

3. On the Uses of Anecdotes

A principal way traditional folk religions accredit, justify, and propagate ideas about the supernatural is by telling and retelling stories. These stories are told to accredit an incredible range of beliefs about spirits, beliefs which vary according to the culture and religion of the teller. A similar epistemological approach undergirds the writings we are examining. Truths are accredited, justified, and propagated by means of anecdotes culled from many sources. A careful reading of Wagner, Jacobs, Kraft, Warner, Murphy, and Otis shows that the stories they tell are not merely intended to illustrate truths arrived at on other grounds, but actually become part of the construction of these truths. They expect us to assent to the validity of the stories and of the inferences drawn from them. Thus, Otis explains that demons are particularly prevalent in mountainous regions. He confirms this by citing the fact that religious belief and practice associate them with mountains and by telling third-hand stories of Christians in Nepal who were bitten, and had food supplies eaten, by demons (1991:89-90). The range of stories from distant places which we are asked to accept range from Warner's account (1991b:129) of a witchdoctor causing a bicycle to burst spontaneously into flames, to Murphy's account (1992:236-237) of long golden needles--demonic power amulets--emerging miraculously from under a shaman's skin through prayer, to Wagner's claim (1988a:83-84, 164-166; 1988b:96) that the most frequent miracle accompanying church growth in Argentina is the miraculous filling of teeth--filled with gold, silver, or white fillings--some with imprints of the cross on them. So common is this miracle, Wagner tells us, that "only those who have had three or more teeth filled or replaced are allowed to give public testimony. One or two teeth are now considered somewhat trivial" (1988a:83).

The use of stories and anecdotes designed to support various doctrines is so pervasive in these writings, and their variety so extensive, that an adequate treatment of such stories would require a book in itself. Because their use is so foundational to the ideas they propose, we will narrow our focus to their use in promoting the doctrine of territorial spirits, and will explore epistemological concerns with the usage of such anecdotes to construct doctrine. For example, Wagner tells of missionary-surgeon-psychiatrist Kenneth McAll who is involved in deliverance ministry:

> As an Anglican he is very much in tune with the power of God channeled through the sacrament of the Eucharist.

> In 1972 McAll and his wife were traveling through the Bermuda Triangle, knowing that many ships and airplanes had disappeared in that area without a trace, and thinking that such a thing could not happen to them. It did. They were overpowered by a fierce storm, the boat was crippled and set adrift, but fortunately they were rescued. McAll discovered through research that in the Bermuda Triangle area the slave traders of a bygone day, in order to collect insurance, had thrown overboard some two million slaves who were too sick or weak to be sold.

> Sensing the leading of God to do something about this, McAll recruited several bishops, priests and others throughout England to celebrate a Jubilee Eucharist in July 1977. Another was held shortly afterward in Bermuda itself. The stated purpose was to seek the "specific release of all those who had met their untimely deaths in the Bermuda Triangle." As a result the curse was lifted, "From the time of the Jubilee Eucharist until now--five years--no known inexplicable accidents have occurred in the Bermuda Triangle" (Wagner 1990:83).

What are we to make of such an account? Wagner's source seems particularly authoritative. McAll combines scientific credentials (he's a surgeon and psychiatrist) with credentials for dealing with spirits (his missionary experience in China). But questions remain. Should one really take the folk belief in a thing called "the Bermuda Triangle" as true, particularly when the books propagating this folk belief have been so thoroughly debunked (cf. Kusche 1975, 1980; Kole and Janssen 1984:82-89; Geisler 1988:49-52)? What exactly is being assumed about the connection between the "untimely" and unjust deaths of these slaves and the present supposed evil mystery? The reference to seeking their "release" suggests that it is the souls of the dead causing the problem. This is, of course, an old animistic idea--that the souls of those who are unjustly killed haunt the spot of their death, bringing danger and death to others. But it is not a biblical position. And what of the use of the Eucharist? Does it not sound somewhat magical?

To verify Wagner's interpretation of McAll, we examined McAll's book (1991). We found that the spirits from which McAll wants to deliver people are not demons, but are the spirits of dead family members and ancestors--people who died without benefit of Eucharist or who died under other evil circumstances. Their souls are believed by McAll to be in an intermediate state where they bother the living. A celebration of the Eucharist, however, delivers their souls to God. And what of the claim that this Eucharist put a stop to the disappearances in the Bermuda Triangle? It certainly has not put a stop to claims of mysterious disappearances. As recently as March of 1993, newspapers across the country reported the mysterious disappearance in the Bermuda Triangle of George and Lynne Drummy and Chuck and Betty Muer with their 40-foot sailboat (see, for example, The Detroit News, March 18, 1993. A, 1:2; A, 6:1,5). Wagner's usage of this account illustrates the way in which narrative accounts invariably have interpretations and assumptions built into them.

Missionaries who accept and propagate such accounts often unwittingly smuggle animistic and magical notions into their understandings of spirit realities. The result is syncretism--in this case, not with enlightenment rationalism, but with animism and magic.

Wagner argues that with respect to issues the Bible does not address--such as whether believers may be demonized--we may legitimately learn from observed experiences (1988a:194). When people question his reports of supernatural events, Wagner suggests that like Flat Earth Society members (1988a:240), such people already have their minds made up and refuse to face the truth. He suggests that just as we accept personal testimonies of salvation as evidence of salvation, so we should accept testimony of other events at face value.   He reasons:

> Suppose an otherwise reasonable person tells me that their teeth were decayed, that someone prayed for them, and that God filled their teeth directly? I look, and sure enough, the teeth are filled. Do I really need dental charts? . . . My current position is that unless I have special reason not to believe it, I take the testimonies of sincere, lucid people at face value. I don't want to be gullible, but I do want to model the attitude advocated by the apostle Paul: love "believes all things" (I Cor 13:7). When there is a choice, I think it is better to be a believer than a skeptic (1988a:242).

But the point to bear in mind for purposes of this paper, is that *we are being asked to accept accounts of events as the epistemological basis for constructing new doctrines about unseen realities.* The issue here is not love and respect for persons, but the epistemological question of what would count as sufficient basis for us to construct new doctrines about unseen spirit realities. After all, Paul warns us not to accept old wives tales, or doctrines of demons, but to test doctrinal claims rigorously (I Tim 4:1,7; I Thess 5:21). Such testing is a biblical demand, not evidence of enlightenment unbelief.[15]

---

[15] When other scholars critique certain of their notions, these authors often invoke the specter of enlightenment rationalism to account for such critiques. Such a rhetorical device allows them to forestall potential criticism of their ideas without having to submit their ideas to public scrutiny and analysis by biblical exegetes, theologians, and Christian anthropologists. In a typical comment, Wagner notes that there have been criticisms of his views, fails to mention what they are, and takes the high road of refusing to "enter into polemics and attempt to refute our critics" (1993a:19). He declares, "We have no inclination to make ourselves look good by making our brothers and sisters in Christ look bad, and you will find none of that in this book" (1993a:19). Then, in the very next paragraph, he characterizes those who reject as unbiblical his ideas on mapping territorial spirits as having knee-jerk reactions similar to those who rejected the Sunday-School movement and the abolition of slavery, comparing them to International Flat Earth Society members (1993a:20). On too many such occasions these authors sidestep substantive debate of critiques leveled against their ideas, discrediting such critiques by assigning pejorative labels to their critics. This is a type of polemic which is unfair to their critics, and avoids the very thing which is needed--

Is it ever possible to infer new extrabiblical understandings of unseen spirits based upon contemporary phenomena? Or should we deny this possibility across the board? The story of the border town street between Uruguay and Brazil has impressed many. Here is an ideal test case, where a missionary actually experimented to see on which side of the street people accepted tracts. But detailed numbers were not kept, and the sample was very small--a few people on a single afternoon. From the purely methodological standpoint, inferences cannot be reliably derived from statistical patterns based on small numbers. Wagner appears to believe this was a recent event (cf. 1988a:201), but in fact this event occurred in 1947, so long ago that the missionary, when contacted by us, could not even remember the name of the town in which it occurred.[16] If territorial spirits really do have such effects, one wonders why for this exact type of account one has to go back 47 years to find one reported instance on a single afternoon in an unknown town.

And is it still not a huge leap from a perceived difference of response on two sides of the street to the inference that it was caused by a territorial spirit whose power can be avoided simply by crossing the street? And how does Wagner harmonize his use of this story with his claims elsewhere that 70% of Brazilians are engaged in spiritism (1988a:187), a statistic which does not seem to fit the notion that the spirits are bound in Brazil? In fact, a highly secular Uruguay has both fewer Christians and fewer spiritists than Brazil. A "territorial spirits" reading of the situation is not clearly indicated by the facts.

If there are conditions by which one may legitimately infer new doctrinal understandings of unseen spirits based on contemporary observed phenomena, these authors neither formulate adequately what such conditions must be, nor inspire one with confidence that this is possible by their own use of such phenomena. We are extremely dubious that this is possible (i.e.,

a direct and honest interchange of ideas and arguments within the context of peer review by other evangelical scholars (missiologists, anthropologists, biblical exegetes, and theologians).

[16] Ralph Mahoney, who is the original written source of this anecdote, in a personal conversation, indicated that the missionary to whom this happened was the Rev. R. Edward Miller. R. Edward Miller essentially confirmed the story, saying that this was part of a four month missions trip to Uruguay in 1947 in which he passed out tracts. On one particular afternoon he was in this border-town, where he had markedly better response on the Brazil side than the Uruguay side. He could not recall the name of the town in which it occurred.

that new doctrine can be validated by any other means than "old doctrine" was validated), but are willing to consider proposals for conditions of such knowledge.

4. The appeal to pragmatism.

These writings often imply that when the effects of certain methods are positive, when the methods "work," such success validates the assumptions on which those methods are based. We can break this issue down into two questions. First, is it clearly established that the effects of the spiritual warfare methods, based on the four assumptions here being critiqued, are positive? Second, do positive results validate the assumptions upon which methods giving such results are based?

First, do such methods and assumptions in fact bring positive results? While the advocates of these methods and assumptions proclaim that they bring great success, one should be cautious about too quickly assuming this to be true. The literature on both shamans and psychotherapists--two other kinds of practitioners whose practical effects have been more carefully studied--makes clear that such practitioners are often more optimistic about the positive effects of their work than an outside objective assessment bears out.[17] Although many studies have measured the results of various counseling techniques, the effects of spiritual warfare types of counseling have not been rigorously measured in a similar fashion. At this point it is simply not known what such a study would reveal. Nor have systematic studies compared the results of evangelistic strategies which feature spiritual warfare based on notions of demonic territoriality with the results of strategies which do not utilize such assumptions.

Furthermore, since the effects to be measured are spiritual ones, such studies would be difficult to carry out. Had

---

[17] Studies of certain problem populations, for example, have shown those receiving counseling under psychotherapists recovering at the same rate as those who received none, or in some cases, particularly with psychoanalytic psychotherapy, recovering at a worse rate than those who received none (Eysenck 1993). That is, it has been demonstrated that some groups (such as cancer patients or juvenile offenders) are actually harmed when treated by psychoanalytic psychotherapy. Yet the psychotherapists involved were convinced that they were helping their patients, as were, in many cases, the patients themselves.

contemporary researchers been present in first century Palestine, one can easily imagine them evaluating positively the responses of thousands at the beginning of John chapter six who rightly recognized Christ as "the Prophet who is to come into the world" and who wanted to make him king (Jn 6:14-15). Yet, researchers would have been wrong to count such people as responding rightly to Christ. For when Christ set forth the true nature of discipleship later in that chapter, their faulty motives for following him were exposed, and all but a handful abandoned him (Jn 6:66). Reliable measures of spiritual ends are difficult, if not impossible, to construct.

If one is to measure the effects of operating with certain assumptions, one must measure all of those effects. One must not only take into account the hundreds of people that Kraft, Warner, or Murphy, for example, have personally counseled. One must also take into account the many thousands who have read their books, taken their courses, listened to their tapes, and passed along such ideas to others. Kraft counseled and exorcised one woman operating on the assumption that a demon had "the right" to inhabit her because she lived in a house where a previous owner had committed adultery (1994b:43). He helped another person who was under demonic influence, he tells us, because a death had once occurred in the house (1994b:43). When he writes about these two instances, however, he has an effect, not on two individuals, but on many readers. These readers now learn that a house where a serious sin or a death has previously occurred may contain demons which have "the right" to inhabit subsequent occupants or owners of the house. And since our world is full of sin and death, it should not surprise us when tens of thousands who are learning this new idea become deeply concerned and fearful that the houses where they live are demonized and need exorcism. These authors are either right to pinpoint an overlooked source of demonic control, or they are unintentionally stimulating the very fears which create a demand for their methods.

Let us assume, however, that many individuals are helped by the methods of Warner, Kraft, and Murphy, and that people of many cities are reached for Christ by Ed Silvoso or John Dawson. Here we raise the second question: Do positive results validate the assumptions upon which the methods giving such results are based? The answer would seem to be "No, not necessarily." On occasion, God works supernaturally even when the method is clearly wrong. Moses was commanded to speak to the rock (Num 20). Instead he struck the rock. His method was clearly wrong and God later punished him. Yet when he struck the rock, God still brought forth water. One would be wrong to infer from a positive result (water miraculously coming from the rock) that the prior human action was thereby validated as the right one.

Seldom, if ever, are all of our assumptions completely accurate. If God failed to act unless all of our methods and assumptions were completely valid, He might seldom act. In fact He has chosen to accommodate Himself to using fallible, error-prone human beings for His own purposes. Ed Silvoso operates with certain assumptions about territorial spirits which we would question. But when he mobilizes all of the churches in a city in an evangelistic campaign which highlights public Christian unity, repentance for ungodly disunity and sin, united prayer, and powerful evangelistic preaching--it is not surprising that many Argentineans listen and respond to the gospel. Silvoso is doing many things right. The gospel is being proclaimed, and fruit results. The resultant fruit, however, does not necessarily validate all of his assumptions. When the results of a given activity are positive, it is not always easy to determine which elements of human strategy and assumptions were critical to such results.[18]

When one method "works," this does not necessarily mean that another method, based on different and contradictory assumptions, might not also "work." Anquash, an Aguaruna Christian, asked, "Do you believe demons can inhabit houses?"[19] "Why do you ask?" the gringo replied. "Well, old man Katan stopped to rest at my house last week when no one was around, and says he saw an *iwanch* (a demon/demonic spirit of the dead) in my house. Now he's telling everyone in the village that my

---

[18] Studies which compare the positive results of one psychotherapy against another (cf. Eysenck 1993, Vitz 1992), for example, have consistently found that 1) theoretically diverse psychotherapies have roughly comparable results, and 2) that what makes the biggest difference in success rates is not the particular set of theories employed by the psychotherapist, but other factors, such as the personal qualities of the psychotherapist (empathy, patience, charisma, interpersonal skills). While many leading psychotherapists believe that their success validates the theories on which they base their methods, objective studies call this assumption into question.

[19] This conversation took place between Robert Priest and a 35 year old Aguaruna Christian, in the village of Tundusa on the Nieva river, early in 1989.

house has an *iwanch.*" The gringo remembered that Anquash's
brother had committed suicide in that house a few years before.
"What do you think?" he asked. "I don't know. I've lived in that
house with my wife and children in peace and happiness. We
read the Bible, sing, and pray. We've never had any problems
with an *iwanch.* I don't understand. It's funny, but I've never
seen an *iwanch.* Have you? . . . Old man Katan [also a Chris-
tian] sees *iwanch* a lot." The conversation went long. Among
other things, the gringo stressed: Satan and demons are real.
The Bible pictures Satan as roving around to do harm. Presumably, then, demons can go anywhere they want to go--
including your house. A Christian's security then, does not
depend on residing in safe places where demons cannot reach us,
but is a security in Christ independent of place. I Corinthians 8
and 10 were discussed. It was suggested that both meat and
houses are part of God's good creation (I Cor 10:26). Merely
physical contact with either is not what makes one vulnerable to
demons. How to claim one's security and resources in Christ
when facing demonic attack were also discussed. Anquash later
expressed deep satisfaction with the ideas he had been presented
with, made use of them in his discussions with others, and the
rumor that his house was haunted soon died out.

But what if a missionary with other assumptions had
counseled Anquash, if it were asserted that houses can be
demonized, that a suicide at a house does bring such demonization, that some Christians (like Katan) have special abilities to
discern such things, and that his house clearly needed to be
exorcised? It is possible that Anquash would have accepted such
counsel and would have moved his family out of the house until
an exorcism could be performed. It is possible that he would
have expressed relief and satisfaction once the house was
exorcised. Two different approaches, based on contradictory
assumptions, may each "work." In such a situation, the issue of
truth, of which assumptions are true, must be settled by recourse
to criteria other than that of pragmatism.

Even when methods "work," they often do so for reasons
other than those assumed by practitioners. When a Christian
with an occult background, for example, fails to get rid of objects
which had occult meanings, associations, or purposes prior to
conversion, it is not uncommon for such failure to be the focus of
spiritual problems. The reason for this, as Paul knew, was that
pre-conversion associations and meanings (related to such objects

as meat offered to idols) are not instantly erased at conversion. Nor can they be erased by a simple verbal correction by another Christian, even if he is an apostle. They are too deeply imbedded. The issue, then, is not the physical object *per se*, but the meanings (in the minds of the relevant individuals) which those objects have for them. When an object has occult meanings for an individual, any failure to repudiate and get rid of the object is indicative of divided spiritual allegiance. And anything which entails divided allegiance, gives Satan an opening and must be renounced. The danger lies, not in physical contact with a physical object, but in how a given individual treats an object which has occult meanings for him. Anything less than repudiation by such a person renders him vulnerable. Given those meanings in the mind of a believing individual, how do we counsel that individual? He or she must repudiate the object and all that it represents. The reason that such a renunciation brings freedom, however, is not that demons need objects to gain power in people. Rather, such a renunciation is an abandonment of a divided allegiance, and the embracing of a single allegiance to God. With that, comes freedom.

There is a difference, however, between adjusting one's methods to "weaker brother" meanings already in a person's mind, and helping to plant such "weaker brother" meanings in a mind that did not formerly think in those terms. The former is appropriate; the latter is not.

Even when the authors here being reviewed implant such ideas in people's minds--rather than adjusting to ideas already in their minds--they may experience seemingly positive results through such methods. This might work, for example, through psychological processes similar to those evident in many rituals of purification around the world (cf. Priest 1993). An Aguaruna man kills another. He experiences a diffuse and all-pervasive fear, guilt, and anxiety--overwhelming feelings for which there is no simple solution. The deed is done, and cannot be undone. Yet continuing life with such overwhelming anxiety is unthinkable. And so, instructed by his culture, he learns to transpose such unfocused anxiety, fear and guilt into a focused concern with blood defilement. That is where the problem lies. By elaborate and arduous rituals designed to remove the defilement, the danger is removed and the anxiety dissipates. Such rituals work, psychologically. The anxiety is alleviated. Similarly, many Christians who feel diffuse anxiety and/or guilt, may be comforted when they are told that their problems are due to a certain object, which they did not realize had occult connections, and which must be removed or exorcised. They may feel a great sense of relief when such an object is removed or exorcised. But while such methods may seem to work psychologically (at least temporarily), if they are not grounded in truth, the resolution cannot be the ideal one. And the new ideas being learned will often bring their own adverse long-term effects (cf. Powlison 1995).

Although the literature on territorial spirits references a number of accounts ostensibly validating the notion of territorial spirits based on pragmatic results, again and again, when the facts can be checked, they are not quite what they seem. For example, Wagner recounts a particularly dramatic exorcism in the Philippines by Assemblies of God evangelist Lester Sumrall, of Clarita Villanueva, a seventeen year old girl who was being bitten by demons. Wagner summarizes Sumrall's account of this event and its after-effects, and comments on it:

> [Prior to this event] after five months of preaching, only five people were saved[20]. . . . Sumrall reports that '150,000 people experienced salvation because of this great miracle' and 'From that day the Philippines has had revival.' I am not sure that we know for a fact whether the power of one or more territorial spirits was broken at that time. But in recent years the rate of church growth has greatly accelerated in the Philippines (Wagner 1991b:44-45).

Hence, a single spiritual victory over a demon purportedly resulted in a changed receptivity to the gospel on the part of a nation. Although Wagner's wording implies that he is cautious and does not want to overstate his case, he nonetheless references this account repeatedly when introducing evidence for the idea of territorial spirits (Wagner 1988a:197-198; 1990:81; 1991b:44-45). It is intended to carry weight with readers.

---

[20] Actually, what Sumrall reports is that "we did not get five people saved." The five who did attend his early sevices included his wife, his three sons, and his servant girl (Sumrall 1986:7).

What is Wagner's source? It is a brief article by Lester Sumrall in a magazine published by the Lester Sumrall Evangelistic Association. When an individual claims that the key to a spiritual breakthrough for a whole nation was himself, minimal caution would suggest that such a claim not be repeated in print until objective verification can be sought. What do the numerous other missionaries to the Philippines think of Sumrall's claim? Wagner suggests that "in recent years the rate of church growth has greatly accelerated in the Philippines" (1991b:45), which, he implies, lends support to such a claim. But while the Sumrall article Wagner references is recent (1986), that article does not make clear that this event actually occured in May of 1953 (cf. Sumrall 1955). It is doubtful that the recently accelerated church growth which Wagner is thinking of relates to the mid-1950's. If one consults Tuggy and Tolliver's book (1972) on church growth in the Philippines, and looks at the charts mapping the growth of the 16 largest protestant churches in the Philippines, one discovers that in 1953 the Assemblies of God (at that time one of the smaller churches) began a period of growth. The Methodists and the United Church of Christ in the Philippines (UCCP), on the other hand, ceased to grow and experienced precipitous declines beginning in 1953. And the rate of the other 13 churches was not altered at all in 1953. There is no evidence here of a nationwide upsurge in evangelistic success-- the one evidence Wagner cites as indicating the defeat of a territorial spirit. There is no evidence that this incident had anything to do with a territorial spirit.

Furthermore, it is Wagner, not Sumrall, who suggests this event might pertain to a territorial spirit. Lester Sumrall attributes his later evangelistic success to the fact that Clarita Villanueva's demonization and subsequent exorcism occured under the spot-light of national media attention. He concludes:

> our work instantly became known all over the
> Philippines. With my picture on the front page of
> newspapers and in magazine stories, people
> would recognize us as we entered places of busi-
> ness or on the streets. It gave us a recognition
> that otherwise would have taken years to receive
> (Sumrall 1955:110-111).

But even Sumrall's 1986 account clearly distorts what actually happened. He writes:

> For the first five months we did not get five people saved. Sometimes I went to church and my wife, my three sons and our servant girl were the only ones in attendance. But I would never let the devil win. Although there were only five, I had church. I both sang and preached. THEN SOMETHING HAPPENED! In Bilibid Prison was Clarita Villanueva. . . . It was a long hard struggle. The devil did not want to let go, but we finally had the victory. . . . 150,000 people experienced salvation because of this great miracle. . . . From that day the Philippines has had revival (Sumrall 1986:7).

This account, however, differs substantially from his own account of events at the time, where he tells supporters that 40 attended his first service, 50 the second, 70 the third, 90 the fourth--with "four sinners" coming forward, and three more conversions the following week (Sumrall 1954:24). A couple of months later Sumrall helped coordinate an evangelistic and healing campaign and reports:

> Twenty thousand souls stood at the invitation for soul salvation. Three hundred and fifty-nine were baptized in water, being the largest baptismal service in the nation's history. Our church is reaping good results. If we had a proper location and a decent building for meetings we could have hundreds more! (Sumrall 1954:25).

Before Clarita Villanueva ever makes her appearance, Sumrall's church was running over 400 in Sunday School (1954:28) and had initiated a bulding program aimed at constructing an edifice which would seat 1500 (1954:28). The claim that he often preached only to his wife, three sons, and servant girl until his encounter with Villanueva's demon, at which time there was a dramatic change, conflicts with his own previous account. Indeed, his third son was not even born until some months after the Clarita Villanueva exorcism (cf 1954:26,36).

This is not the kind of report that one can rely on to validate ideas about territorial spirits.   While Wagner's published accounts of this event, together with the interpretation that it led to a nationwide surge in converts, might naturally lead readers to agree that a territorial spirits interpretation of this event is the most viable and persuasive hypothesis, that interpretation does not fit the facts. Wagner is clearly less than adequately careful in his use of sources.

The epistemological issue of pragmatic results is, in a real sense, purely hypothetical. Despite the fact that Wagner and Kraft call for field research which would form the basis for a "science" of the demonic, no research findings--as to practical results--which pass even the most elementary requirements of research design are currently in print lending support to any of the four doctrines here being critiqued. Our discussion here does not concern established studies; such do not exist. It concerns, rather, the hypothetical possibility that a research design could be developed which would allow such doctrines to be established (or falsified) through field research.   For reasons already adduced, we are extremely skeptical that such is even hypothetically possible. The relevant variables (1. an object or territory with a demon attached, for example, and 2. spiritual effects of contiguity) pose intractable problems for operationalizing them with adequate reliability and validity.   Creating controlled conditions which would rule out other explanations of the results would be difficult. Perhaps the biggest problem relates to the fact that the subject matter concerns personal beings, rather than impersonal forces or processes. Psychologists, who also study personal beings, find that research requires the willing cooperation of subjects and/or their ignorance of what the psychological test is attempting to measure.   If the subjects understand what the test is attempting to measure, and they are so inclined, they may respond in the light of that knowledge to intentionally sabotage and distort the results. While humans often willingly cooperate and can be kept in the dark as to the specific variables the test is attempting to measure, neither of these is true of demons. There is no reason to believe that such a test could be constructed without the full awareness of demons. Demons, of course, are not interested in cooperating with our quest for information.   Their goal, rather, is disinformation. Such a study, we suspect, would provide an optimum opportunity for them to manipulate the results, helping to accredit falsehoods as truths.

We do not believe, then, that the test of pragmatism provides an adequate epistemological basis for establishing new truth about unseen spirits and the nature of their powers.

5. *Inner Geiger Counters*

A Geiger counter is an instrument which may be used to detect otherwise unobservable objects by their ionizing particles. The authors we are critiquing often write as if spirits create an invisible force field and as if people had inner Geiger counters which allow them to detect the presence of unseen demonic spirits. Otis, for example, tells us, "Many Christian travelers have had the experience of crossing the threshold of a particular country, province, city or neighborhood only to find that the prevailing atmosphere has suddenly turned oppressive" (1992:86). Later he argues that "almost everyone" has had such an experience (1993:36). He tells of experiences of this type which he has had, experiences from which he infers the presence of territorial spirits in certain regions. Just as we have natural senses to observe the physical material world, so he suggests, we have "spiritual senses" (1992:86) which allow us to detect territorial spirits. He concludes, "While some individuals elect to shrug off these negative feelings as subjective mood swings, more and more Christians are coming to the realization that what they are experiencing is related directly to the presence and influence of unseen territorial spirits" (1992:87). Otis contends that negative feelings experienced when entering certain territories are based on spiritual senses which accurately perceive the presence of demonic spirits, and that we may then use such feelings as a basis for making inferences about unseen spirit realities. Such feelings give evidence that territorial spirits exist and may be used to help map such spirits (see also Otis 1993:36). Others also promote the inner Geiger counter idea. Dawson reports, "Often when I first arrive in a new location, I discern the unseen realm most clearly because I sense the contrast in atmosphere between the old location and the new" (1989:153). He tells us that in Belo Horizonte, Brazil, "you can sense victory in the heavenlies" (1991a:xi), while he discovered that Manaus "was oppressed by a dominating, contentious spirit" with other spirits working under it (1991a:xi).   Cindy Jacobs tells of discerning "four major ruling, territorial spirits" over Mar del Plata, Argentina (Jacobs 1991:102).   Likewise Sterk reports that "in an animistic Indian village where I lived and worked in southern Mexico . . . the ominous domination of that area was so oppressive that we could literally feel it" (1991:148).

In some cases there is the notion that people with prior exposure to the occult are particularly sensitive to these realities and can be counted on to discern truth. Thus Ed Murphy says,

> As is often the case with believers who have been "demonized," set free, and gone on to a close walk with the Lord, Carolyn became quite sensitive to the spirit world. She is acutely aware of the presence of evil spirits in people and places, even in homes and stores (Murphy 1992:521).

And while former U.S. Secretary of the Interior, James Watt, lost his job, in part, because of lack of sensitivity to minorities, Wagner tells of a different kind of sensitivity which he believes Watt has. Watt, Wagner (1990:80) says, "through sensitivities acquired in his past association with the occult, perceives specific dark angels assigned to the White House." Wagner then points to the significant implications of such "insights."

How should we evaluate such an idea that some, or all, of us can "sense" the presence of the demonic?   That we can extrapolate from our feelings to inferences about unseen spirit realities, inferences which take us beyond that which is revealed in Scripture? Does the Bible give any support to the idea that we have a natural capacity or spiritual gifting to emotionally sense and accurately perceive the demonic? No. Passages refering to testing the spirits and to discernment of spirits speak of discernment and testing based upon doctrine, not of a free-floating emotional Geiger-counter which will automatically go off when in the presence of the demonic.[21]

---

[21] The Apostle John says that believers test the spirits by listening to what people say about Jesus Christ (I Jn 4:1-6). The apostolic testimony is the means by which one discerns the presence of the Spirit of God or the spirit of antichrist. Paul concurs. Satan's approach is to tell lies about Jesus. God's Word exposes the lies, and hence the presence of the satanic, providing the antidote for those deceived (II Cor 4:3-6; 11:3-4). Paul introduces his discussion of spiritual gifts by

On one occasion a traveling missionary spent the night in an Aguaruna village.[22]   He asked if there were any Christians in the village.   When informed that not only did no Christians live in the village, but that they had required all Christians to get off their village land, the missionary spent a restless, sleepless night.   Shortly after this he reported to other missionaries that while in this village he could "sense" the presence and power of the evil one.   Another missionary who had worked in this area was shocked, and declared, "that village has a strong and vibrant church."   "But I asked and they told me there were no Christians in the village," he replied.   "What exactly did you ask? . . . Ah, you should have asked if they had a church, if any were believers, if any had a Bible.   The word for Christian which you used was a word the Hispanic conquerors used of themselves, a word which, for the Aguaruna, has come to simply mean a mestizo.   What you really asked them was if any mestizos lived in their village.   None do.   But lots of believers in Jesus Christ live there."

When missionaries assert, as they commonly do, that in a certain region they could sense the power of Satan, or palpably sense the spiritual darkness, this should not be understood as an independent capacity to directly and reliably perceive whether or not demons are present.   This is not to deny that demons can directly attack emotions, only that if they can and do, it is at their discretion and initiative.   We should not expect demons to obligingly send such a signal each time they are present and active.   We are naive to assume that the presence or absence of such emotions is a reliable indicator of the presence or absence of demons and to use such emotions to map such demons or to infer their presence or absence in object or place.   Furthermore, our

---

telling his readers how to discern what "spirit" is present, namely, by listening to what that person says about Jesus Christ (I Cor 12:1-3).   And while the gift of "distinguishing of spirits" is not specifically defined in this passage (I Cor 12:10), given its relationship to the speaking gift of "prophecy" (I Cor 12:10)--a relationship exemplified in I Cor 14:29-33--and to what Paul has just indicated as the basis of discerning whether a spoken word is by the Spirit of God, it seems clear that this passage is referring to a gift of discerning the implications of what people **say** about Jesus Christ and not to a gift of emotionally **sensing** the presence of invisible demonic spirits (cf., II Thess 2:2-5).   Practice in understanding and applying the truth of the Word of God is the means of discernment for the mature believer (Heb 5:14).

[22] The Aguaruna are an Amazonian Indian group with whom Robert Priest conducted fieldwork from 1987-1989.

capacity to know for sure whether such emotions are caused by demons or by other factors is suspect. This is because many things can cause or contribute to such emotions. Sickness and culture shock are two such causes often experienced by missionaries at the very time they are encountering new religions, ways of life, people, and places. Missionaries see people who do not worship God, people who scorn the things they hold sacred, strange cultural and religious practices, strange music, behavior deemed shockingly immoral, etc., and it is not surprising that disturbed feelings result--feelings which sometimes lead them to speak in terms of being able to "sense" the spiritual darkness. But in such cases this should be understood, not as an epistemological feat of directly perceiving the demonic, but as an inference based on what they do perceive, and on the disturbed feelings which result from such perceptions.

John Dawson often writes of sensing the demonic, or of feeling demonic oppression, drawing inferences from this sensing. But a careful reading of Dawson suggests that his feelings might well be explainable in terms of natural perceptions of observed phenomena. Thus, for example, he writes of a neighborhood where "demonic oppression almost crushed my soul" (1989:29). In the same context, however, he tells of receiving death threats, of having his tires slashed, and of the depressing "sight of boarded-up houses, unemployed youth, and disintegrating families" (1989:29). The authors of this paper have had comparable experiences, where being in certain contexts gave us marked feelings of despondency, gloom, anxiety, and demoralization. Where we differ from the authors being examined is in the conviction that we cannot read those feelings as giving us a direct and reliable perception of the demonic, from which we may cognitively derive inferences about such unseen realities, particularly inferences with truth implications not given in Scripture. There is no biblical basis for inferring new understandings of spirits based on such feelings.

6. Personal Revelations from God

Kraft argues that God continues to give special "words of knowledge" about specific situations which we face. He writes:

> Words of knowledge usually come to me feeling
> like hunches or guesses. Other people get them
> in a variety of ways. Sometimes they feel a pain
> somewhere in their body indicating that someone
> needs to be prayed over for a physical problem in
> that part of the body. . . . Sometimes a word will
> come as a picture, often as a picture of some part
> of a person's body that needs to be prayed over
> (Kraft 1989:158).

Kraft acknowledges there is risk in acting on "something
that feels as vague as most of my God-given insights." "But," he
continues, "though I make quite a few mistakes, the vast
majority of these 'hunches' turn out to be from God" (Kraft
1989:159). Cindy Jacobs describes contemporary revelation in
similar terms (1991:75), also acknowledging that it is not easy to
distinguish God's voice from other voices. She says:

> When we listen to the spirit of God . . . it is very
> much like turning on the television. There are
> many channels on that TV, but not all the chan-
> nels come from the Holy Spirit. Simply because
> we have tuned into a channel and hear a voice
> does not mean that it is the voice of God
> (1991:85).

She goes on to explain that "all of us" need to submit
such revelations to others for testing.

Peter Wagner distinguishes the *logos* word of God, God's
eternal written word in the Scriptures, from the *rhema* word of
God, God's immediate personal word about a pointed situation
(1991a:15-16). The former is inerrant, while the latter is not. He
understands "words of knowledge" under the latter category (see
also Wagner 1988a:230ff).

But what is clear from each of these authors is that many
people think they are picking up such a revelation, and are
mistaken. That is, these authors make no claim to receive
revelations without error. So the validity of such truth claims
must be established on other grounds. The primary thrust of
such claims to revelation is to perceive something about specific
situations. In Wagner's terms (1988a:231), "they allow us to

understand more specifically just what the Father is doing" in situations such as a sickness.

We do not dispute that God can and does give special insight to individuals concerning special situations. We do question whether God is continuing to give special revelation. Insight does not add new doctrine. New revelation does. When some of these authors occasionally claim insight based on private words of knowledge--insight with truth implications about the supernatural not given in Scripture--and propagate such doctrinal implications in the public arena, we should be clear that it is new revelation which is being claimed. But if God expects the church at large to accept such new doctrinal understandings, then the prophets involved must meet the tests of the prophet--they must not make mistakes in any of their claimed revelations and their claim to revelation must be backed by genuine miracle signs.[23]

7. *Appeals to Scripture*

While the authors in view appeal largely to extrabiblical reasoning and evidence in support of the four doctrines we are examining, they do attempt to link the doctrines to Scripture and do cite specific passages in support of their doctrines. However, the connection between the references they cite and the doctrine for which they seek biblical support is often oblique and but superficially suggestive. Alternate interpretations are rarely entertained. They seem to disregard clear passages which do not agree with their assertions. Before ending this paper we must look carefully at the way they use Scripture to support such doctrines. Does Scripture, in fact, teach these doctrines?

---

[23] cf. Deut. 13:1ff. While Wagner and Kraft both claim to have the gift of lengthening legs, this does not seem overly impressive, particularly when Kraft acknowledges that in many cases the lengthened leg is as a result of muscle relaxation rather than growth (1989:91). Wagner himself distinguishes miracles from healings and acknowledges that his own healings do not fall in the category of miracle (1995:57-58). Neither Wagner nor Kraft claim that their words of revelation are without error. Kraft on one occasion, for example, felt he had a message about the grandchildren of a woman who, it turned out, was not a grandmother (Kraft 1989:160).

A. *Demonic transmission through objects*

When Kraft, Murphy, Wagner, and Warner assert that demonic influence and power is transmitted through contact with certain physical objects, they do so largely on extra-biblical grounds. However they do occasionally appeal to the Bible in support of this doctrine. In defence of the idea that demonic influence is transmitted through objects, these authors develop two lines of argument. They argue, first, that the Bible directly teaches this--a claim we will critique shortly. Second, they argue that this pattern is evident in the way God uses objects, that Satan and God operate essentially under the same set of rules (cf. Kraft 1994b:42), and that we may infer from God's use of objects something about the demonic use of objects. We will address the second argument first, breaking the issue down into two questions: (1) Do these authors accurately understand God's use of material objects when his miraculous power is exercised? and (2) what may we legitimately infer about the demonic use of objects from God's use of objects?

Kraft (1994b:47) argues that God invests places and things with power and cites the Ark of the Covenant (1 Sam 4-7), Jesus' garment (Mt 9:20), and Paul's handkerchiefs and aprons (Acts 19:11-12) as biblical examples of this. In fact, the list of objects, actions, and words which play a key role in God's supernatural activity could be extended much further. Aaron stretched his rod over the Nile to turn it to blood (Ex 7:19-20). Moses stretched his rod over the Red Sea to open a path (Ex 14:16,21) and struck the rock at Horeb with it to bring forth water (Ex 17:6). Elijah took his cloak, struck the Jordan river with it, and the river parted (2 Kgs 2:8). Elisha used Elijah's cloak to do the same (2 Kgs 2:14). Elisha cut a stick and threw it in the water to cause the axe head to float (2 Kgs 6:6). Jesus spoke to a storm: "Peace, be still! (Mk 4:39)" He mixed saliva and mud to heal blind eyes (Jn 9:6,7). Moses's rod, Elijah's cloak, Elisha's bones (2 Kgs 13:21), Jesus' garment, Jesus' saliva, and Paul's handkerchiefs and aprons were all physical objects or substances which were brought into contiguity or contact with persons or objects which were then supernaturally changed.

Kraft is not wrong, then, when he detects certain parallels between the use of such objects in biblical narratives and their use in magic/animism. Both in magic and in biblical miracle contiguity and/or symbolic association are present. Jesus often touched people when he healed them. Or he spoke. Or he applied his own saliva to a mute tongue (Mk 7:33-34) or to blind eyes (Mk 8:23).

The function of contiguity or symbolic association in biblical miracle, however, is quite different from its function in magical or animistic thought. In magic and animism the assumption is that contiguity and symbolic association are themselves the key to power, its transmission, and its effects. Without contiguity and symbolic association, power is inoperative. In Scripture, however, there is no indication that God required such means for His power to be operative. In the Bible such associations are there, not because they are necessary for power to operate, but because they are an appropriate and helpful accommodation to communication and interaction with human beings.

In the Bible miracles are called "signs," suggesting that they are communicative acts. Communicative acts require indexical or symbolic markers if communication is to occur. Jesus could have stilled the storm without uttering a word or moving a muscle. But in that case the event would simply have seemed strange and inexplicable. The disciples would not have known that Jesus did it. To communicate that a supernatural act was intended, there needed to be a visible action or sign connecting the emissary with the miracle. These acts are communicative acts--designed to demonstrate a linkage between the miracle event and God's emissary--and carry specific implications, minimally, that this person is (or was) God's special prophet or apostle and that the message, therefore, should be believed.

God also often required human communicative acts-- external displays of faith and obedience--as a condition for God's miraculous acts. Joshua and the Israelites were commanded to march around Jericho and blow their trumpets (Josh 6:3-5). Snake-bit Israelites were asked to look at a brass serpent (Num 21:8-9). Naaman was instructed to bathe seven times in the Jordan river (2 Kgs 5:10), and the man born blind was instructed to wash mud-smeared eyes at the pool of Siloam (Jn 9:7). One should not assume that the efficacy for Naaman's healing resided in the waters of the Jordan, or that the fall of Jericho lay in how many times the Israelites marched around Jericho. Rather, the external acts provided people a means of responding and demonstrating faith, both to themselves and to others. Similarly, when the woman touched Jesus' garment and was healed, the significant thing to learn from her touch is that she had faith in Jesus and was healed, not that physical contact with a physical object physically in contact with Jesus is a natural means of tapping into power. The human display of faith often involves actions with imagery of contiguity and/or symbolic association. But again, in the Bible, what is key is the faith; the outward acts merely demonstrate the inward response. In magic and animism it is the external forms--the objects and symbols themselves-- which are key.

When, on one occasion, people of Ephesus--impressed by Paul's healing ministry--carried his handkerchiefs and aprons to sick people who were healed, it is unclear as to whether this was being done with Paul's approval and consent. What is clear is that God was performing these miracles to accredit Paul and his message. The method was one in which more people were healed than could have been visited in person by Paul. The handker-chiefs and aprons served indexically to link Paul to these widespread healings, thus accrediting Paul and his message before a wider audience than he might otherwise have had. When Luke characterizes these particular miracles as τυχουσας variously translated "special" (AV), "singular" (NEB), "remarkable" (JB) or "extraordinary" (RSV, NIV)--it would seem that Luke is drawing attention to the uniqueness of the miracles on this occasion. What we should not infer is that this incident is intended as a normative pattern to be adopted for the transmis-sion of power. Indeed, God's acts in Scripture repeatedly seem to be designed to preclude the notion that words, objects, and physical actions are themselves the key to the miraculous event. The blind people healed by Jesus, for example, were healed with various physical actions accompanying the healing. On occasion Jesus touched blind eyes (Mt 9:29; 20:34), applied spittle (Mk 8:23), simply spoke (Lk 18:42; My 10:52), or applied mud (Jn 9:6). Such variability in Jesus' methods would seem to be highlight-ing the fact that the key to these healings was not the particular technique or physical object or substance involved, but the person of Christ. The point is not that rituals and objects have power, but that Jesus has power.

Kraft suggests that God empowers objects. When super-natural consequences of using or misusing such objects are evident, it is due to the "force-field" power infusing such objects.

Such power is directly operative in accordance with laws governing its effects. The power is God's power, just as electrical power is God's. God created each. But once they are brought into existence they operate in accord with their own law-governed properties, and not in accord with the independent initiative of God on each occasion. The Ark of the Covenant, Kraft (1994b:55) affirms, was an "empowered item" which caused "great disruption" among the Philistines (I Sam 5). But the Bible, here, does not teach the idea of a "force-field" power attached to the Ark, causing such disruption. Rather, it says, "Now the hand of the Lord was heavy on the Ashdodites, and He ravaged them and smote them (I Sam 5:6). Again, in I Sam 6:19 and II Sam 6:7, when people peered into or touched the Ark and were killed, the text itself stresses the anger and initiative of God in killing them, rather than that contact with a powerful force-field killed them. II Sam 6:7, for example, says, "And the anger of the Lord burned against Uzzah, and God struck him there for his irreverence." God had assigned special meaning to the Ark. When people displayed disrespect for the Ark, they were, in effect, displaying disrespect for God. And God took appropriate action.

On occasion people in the Bible did come to think magically about objects and places. The sons of Eli treated the Ark of the Covenant as a power object, and took it to battle assuming its physical presence would give them victory (1 Sam 4). Jonah connected God with a place, and tried to flee from His presence. The Israelites took the bronze serpent and burned incense to it (2 Kgs 18:4)--apparently assuming the object itself was the key to the supernatural power which had been operative when snake-bit people looked at it and were healed (Num 21:8-9). The sons of Sceva treated the name of Jesus as a magic word, and believed that it--the word rather than the person--would give them power (Acts 19:13-16).

Human communication and thought invariably use metaphor and metonymy. Magic treats metaphor and metonymy, not as communicative devices, but as devices for the transmission of power--necessary circuits for a kind of supernatural electricity. Just as science deals with forces such as electricity, and must employ appropriate conductors if that electricity is to be operative, so magic postulates powers which require contiguity (metonymy) or symbolic association (metaphor) for the power to be transmitted and to have its effects. In the Bible, however, such associations are there, not because they are necessary for power to operate, but because they are a critical component of communication and interaction. They are present not because of a need to accommodate to limitations in God's power, but because God chose to use them to accommodate Himself to human communication and thought.

Kraft (1992:198,231; 1994b:47) teaches that we can bless objects or substances such as water, oil, or salt, that such substances are then imbued with God's power, and that we may then employ those substances to exorcise demons from houses or people. Such ideas, we suggest, are more magical than biblical. This paper, however, concerns demonic power in relation to objects--not God's power in relation to objects. We discuss God's use of objects in this paper, not in order to reflect on how Christians should or should not seek to empower objects (a possible topic for another paper), but to examine what may or may not be inferred about demonic use of objects from God's use of objects.

Since God uses objects in connection with His communicative acts, then it should not surprise us if objects play a role in Satan's deceptive activity. Specific objects may be infused with evil meanings in the minds of specific people--meanings which are false and/or which seductively appeal to their lust, covetousness and pride and which direct them away from God and the good. When those people act wrongly toward such objects based on these meanings which the objects have for them, Satan has power in the lives of those people--just as he always has power in the lives of those whom he successfully deceives, tempts, and seduces. But it is altogether a different matter to infer that the object itself transmits power; that quite apart from its meaning for the individual and quite apart from any associated wrong cognitive, moral, or spiritual response on the part of the individual, its mere physical presence creates a vulnerability to demonic power--a vulnerability not otherwise present. It is this to which we object. And it is this which simply cannot be inferred from God's use of objects in Scripture. The evidence advanced by the authors examined in this paper is inadequate to support the idea that if Satan or demons can first get connected with an object (perhaps with the help of some third party) and then bring the object in physical contact with a person, that quite apart from any meaning it may have for that person, they can exercise greater power over that person than would be possible in the absence of the object. If God's use of objects demonstrated A: that God's power is increased by the use of objects, then perhaps one could entertain inference B: that demonic power is increased by the use of objects. But if A is untrue, as it is, then B cannot be inferred from A. God may be more likely to act where human response is right. Satan may be more able to act where human response is wrong. But the presence or absence of physical objects in no way affects God's power to act. Therefore, we cannot infer from God's use of objects that the mere physical presence of any objects in proximity to an individual enhances demonic power over that individual.

But if we cannot infer from God's use of objects, that objects are critical to demonic power, perhaps the Bible directly addresses the issue of demons and objects. Here these authors cite a few passages--passages which, it seems to us, they read through the lens of a magical/animistic worldview.[24]   Warner (1994:30-31) summarizes his argument from these passages:

> God made it plain that His people should not bring certain religious objects into their homes. They were, in fact, to detest and burn them (Deut 7:25-26). Evil spirits can use such objects as a medium to come to people (Deut 32:17, Ps 106:37, I Cor 10:19-20).

After citing Wagner to the effect that demons can infect objects, and through objects, the people who come in contact with them, John Robb (1994:182-3) exclaims:

---

[24] See our definitions of animism and magic earlier in this paper. Some have suggested that when words like animism or magic are used to characterize beliefs or practices, such words carry no specific cognitive content, only affect. That is, one condemns by applying labels appealing to negative affect but lacking cognitive content. (For a clear example of such a view, see Garrett 1989:4.) We, however, have provided specific substantive definitions for what we mean by the terms. In this respect we make three claims. First, animism and magic, as practiced in the cultures of the world, rest in large part on two assumptions about how it is that (spirit) power is operative (i.e., that the principle of contiguity/contagion and the principle of similarity/imitation are assumed to be the bases upon which such power is operative). Second, these assumptions about how it is that demonic power is operative diverge from Biblical ones. Third, these authors are teaching people to think about demonic power in terms of these two assumptions. Only if we are wrong at any one of these three points, would our usage of these terms to characterize certain ideas of these missiologists be inappropriate.

No wonder God through Moses commanded Israel not to bring any "detestable things" into their homes because of the destructive effects they would bring upon them. The ruthless actions of reformer kings like King Josiah to rid the land of the high places, shrines, and other occult objects used in the worship of foreign gods are now fully understandable (Dt 7:25-26; II Kgs 23).

Wagner puts it this way:

Deuteronomy 32:17 and I Corinthians 10:19-20, for instance, clearly associate idols with demons. This is why idolatry is so categorically condemned in the Bible. Idols are nothing. Pieces of wood or stone are no threat to the kingdom of God. The real threats are the demonic personalities that have attached themselves to the idols, most frequently at the invitation of humans (in Archer 1994:56).

Elsewhere Wagner (1992:78) says:

objects such as physical idols have the potential to harbor incredibly malignant power. This is, I believe, what is behind the first two of the Ten Commandments: "You shall have no other gods before me" and "You shall not make for yourself any graven image" (Exod 20:3,4).

When Wagner argues that the reason for the first two commandments, the reason "why idolatry is so categorically condemned in the Bible" is because idolatry brings one into contact with objects which have demons attached to them, Wagner would seem to be reading Scripture through the lens of an animist world view. The Bible says that people who worship money, or people whose god is their belly, are idolaters just as those who bow before wooden statues. The reason God condemns idolatry is clearly stated. It is not because of potential magical contagion of demons, but because God alone is to be worshipped. The threat held over idolaters is not that they will "pick up" a demon, but that God is a jealous God. When God told the Old Testament Israelites not even to touch objects used by pagans in religious worship, He was not addressing people whose tendency was to be skeptical of other religions and whose skepticism might lead them into careless physical contact with some object, thus contaminating them or their children with a demon. Rather, the prohibition was addressed to people who tended repeatedly to be seduced into the belief in and worship of other gods, and who were inclined to attribute the same supernatural connotations to those objects which their pagan neighbors did and to act towards such objects in accord with pagan religious assumptions and motivations.

A straightforward exegesis of I Corinthians 8 and 10 makes clear that these authors are wrong. When Kraft asserts, "artifacts dedicated to enemy gods (spirits) have demons in them" (Kraft 1992:112), implying that artifacts transmit demons, he contradicts Scripture. He is taking an animist principle and asserting it as doctrine. It is not that Kraft is necessarily wrong in saying that a demon <u>can</u> enter an object, but that he is wrong in what he implies by that. We know of nothing which would restrict demons from being anywhere they want to be. We do not, strictly speaking then, deny that a demon can enter an object or inhabit the same space as an object. What we deny is that the demon gains a tactical advantage by doing so--that by entering meat, let us say, the demon is able to enter and gain a power over the person who happens to eat the meat, a power not otherwise available. Paul denies that physical contact with a physical object, previously dedicated to an idol, carries with it any intrinsic danger. This is the belief of the weaker brothers whose prior paganism had "so accustomed" them to such a framework of thought, that even as Christians they could not shake themselves free from it. Under animistic thinking, objects or substances which are ingested have the greatest potential for transmitting supernatural influences. Other objects sit on the shelf, or at most come in contact with one's outer skin. But objects which are ingested, such as meat which has been offered to an idol, are taken directly into one's body. Yet Paul is very clear. If a physical object, meat in this case, has been offered to a pagan deity, and a Christian is later fed this meat, the Christian need not have the slightest fear that his contact with the meat will contaminate him or his children with demons. This passage directly contradicts the animist principle being propagated by these authors. If a gift is offered, whether of a doll or of food, one should accept it, ask no questions, fear no results. One may touch such gifts, bring them into one's home, and even into one's own body, with the confidence that physical contact with physical objects does not, in itself, render one vulnerable to demonic influence or power. Of course, if one uses such objects with (non-Christian) religious meanings and purposes in mind, that is another matter altogether.

Paul warns of two dangers: 1.) First, one may eat meat previously offered to idols in such a way that others may stumble. On the one hand, weaker brothers may be tempted to eat despite having understandings which make the eating a violation of conscience. On the other hand, unbelievers could interpret your eating as a compromise of your public witness and testimony. 2.) The second danger is that of participating in a religious activity of worship--something which Paul says involves us in communion with demons--which a jealous God will not tolerate. Both of these biblically explicitly stated dangers are fundamentally different from the putative danger asserted by the animist doctrine--that we are vulnerable to demonic influence and power based on our physical contact with objects formerly dedicated to other supernatural beings.

B. Curses

Animistic or magical thinking asserts that if one can manipulate one thing which symbolically stands for another, you can magically manipulate that other thing. If you can make an image of someone, and stick a needle through it, you can harm that person. Related to this is the widespread belief that words which symbolically stand for things can also be manipulated magically so as to harm that for which they stand. Thus one's name may be a closely guarded secret, on the belief that someone can verbally do something with the name (i.e., make some evil pronouncement which harms the person tied to that name). Thus one word, "death" for example, may be juxtaposed to another, "Bill," by use of a verbal formula and accompanied by rituals with the expectation that this will cause Bill to die. "Verbal magic," anthropologists have observed, is a subset of "sympathetic magic," based on the same principles of thought.

These authors appeal to Scriptures to validate "verbal magic." But since there is no biblical teaching linking demonic power with curses, these authors again develop their argument in terms of God's use of blessings and curses. They show how God, various of the patriarchs, and Jesus make pronouncements of blessings and cursings which come to pass. Their notion of a kind of natural efficacy to curses, whether invoked by occultists or Christians, is animistic, not biblical. God, or God through His spokespeople, may choose to exercise His power in certain contexts by verbal curses, by touch, or by mixing saliva with mud and applying it to blind eyes. But the Bible never teaches that the power resides in the formula or in the technique or in some other impersonal object. The power is God's. And while God may choose to exercise his power in the context of a limited technique on occasion, we cannot infer from this the opposite principle--that Satan and his minions have their power to harm certain people enhanced by the usage of ritual techniques by other humans.[25] Nor may we infer that there is some independent source of magical power which curses tap into. When Kraft, for example, claims that we have God's power to back up curses, but then warns that we not use that power wrongly (1992:76), he implies that the power is now our own. We can use it to harm illegitimately and independently of God's will. Jacobs makes this explicit, though in the following passage she refers to these verbal pronouncements as bindings rather than curses:

> Some people run around and "claim" houses and property, which puts bindings on other people's property. We have known people who were unable to sell property for long periods of time because some Christian decided that he wanted it as his own and prayed accordingly. . . . When someone prays a prayer out of his own mind, will or emotion, he is releasing tremendous psychic (and many times demonic) forces to work against the one for whom he is praying. Proverbs 18:21

---

[25] This notion that human magical actions increase demonic power appears occasionally in the literature. For example, Jacobs contends: "The territorial spirits over a city or region *are greatly empowered* by the occult spells, curses, rituals and fetishes used by witches, warlocks and satanists (1993:86, italics added).

says: Death and life are in the power of the tongue (Jacobs 1991:138).

Two assumptions often appear. One is that the power being accessed is an impersonal power, or a power located in people (i.e., psychic power) and is thus used independently of the will of God or of evil spirits. Just as God created forces such as electricity, He created spiritual forms of power such as cursing. Like electricity, once such powers are in existence, they may be employed towards one's own variable ends. This is not a biblical notion. It is animistic and magical. And it is through the lens of animism and magic that Jacobs has read Proverbs 18:21. That is, this passage is speaking of words used in normal ways. It is not establishing a doctrine about the independent power of words used for magical purposes.

An alternative assumption is that the power is demonic, but that human rituals and conjurations enhance the power of demons to act towards others in harmful ways. Again, there is no biblical grounds for such a doctrine. We do not deny the power of demons. We contend, however, that human beings cannot add to their power or their desire to harm others. And since the doctrine is often coupled with the doctrine that objects can mediate demons (i.e., the reason objects have demons is because of curses and conjurations, and the way the curse is transmitted is through an object[26]), Paul's robust denial that we need to fear contact with objects also contradicts the doctrine of curses mediating demonic influence and danger. Proverbs 26:2 explicitly tells us that a curse which is undeserved should not be feared. If we have done something to deserve a curse, such as defraud a widow or orphan, then we should fear--not the natural efficacy of an old woman's verbal pronouncements--but the anger and retribution of a righteous God who protects widows and orphans. But if a shaman or some member of the occult curses us, then "like a sparrow in its flitting, like a swallow in its flying" such a curse "does not alight." To teach Christians to fear the demonic consequences of the verbal pronouncements of others is to teach them an animist doctrine, not a biblical one.

---

[26] When writing of "the empowerment of cultural forms such as words, material objects, places and buildings" by demons, Kraft stresses, "The empowerment of words is basic to this whole section. Words usually serve as the vehicle through which other items are empowered" (Kraft 1994b:54).

C. *The Genealogical Transmission of Demons*

The Bible teaches that all human beings are sinners from conception (Ps 51:5). Each child enters the world having inherited from parents and ancestors--all the way back to Adam-- an ungodly affinity with sin and evil which renders them subject to Satan. This inherited condition is universal and applies to all.

What these authors argue is that there is also a condition selectively inherited by some children, but not all--a condition of inherited demonic control. The belief that demons can attach to unborn babies because of some contact the parent has had, or some activity they have engaged in, is a doctrine which occasionally appears in animistic religions. The Bible does not address this issue. The only biblical passages to which supporters of the doctrine appeal are passages speaking of God "visiting the iniquity of the fathers on the children, on the third and fourth generation of those who hate me" (Exodus 20:5; 34:7). They argue that God punishes the third and fourth generation because demons which were attached to their fathers, causing those sins, were transmitted to the children by genealogical inheritance, thus causing them to commit the same sins (cf., White 1994:36; Anderson 1991:227; Murphy 1992:437-8; Kraft 1994a:88). This is an enormous leap of inference, sustainable only if one first assumes that the doctrine in question is true. This passage simply does not teach anything about the potential of unborn children picking up demons because of their parents' occult activities or contacts with occult objects.

If we wonder how it is that children often end up with the same sins as their parents, we need not resort to undisciplined speculations. The Bible itself points to the role of parents in teaching and modeling and carries solemn warnings to those who lead children astray or cause them to stumble. Direct parental influence, then, is what is key. Such influence is a moral influence, not a magical one. "The parents have eaten sour grapes, and the children's teeth are set on edge" (Jer 31:29; Ez 18:2), declared an old Israeli proverb. But Jeremiah (31:29-30) and Ezekiel (18:2-4) vigorously repudiated such a notion: "For every living soul belongs to me [God], the father as well as the son--both alike belong to me. The soul who sins is the one who will die" (Ez 2:4). "Whoever eats sour grapes--his own teeth will be set on edge" (Jer 31:30). A wicked parent may set an evil precedent and example, but the son is punished only if he follows that example--something which is not causally determined (Ez 18).

When an adopted child is told, 'Your biological ancestor was involved in some occult activity and thereby gave demons ownership over you so that you were demonized from conception,' this seems both to be a denial that "every living soul" belongs to God (Ez 2:4) and to be a modern version of that ancient heterodox proverb: "The father's have eaten sour grapes, and the children's teeth are set on edge."

This doctrine rests, finally, on extra-biblical principles of inference (such as words of knowledge, demonic revelations, anecdotes, and native beliefs). These, we have already shown, are inadequate epistemological bases for constructing new doctrines. This doctrine, along with the two preceding it, rests on the animistic assumption that our vulnerability to demonic influence derives from physical or symbolic contact or contiguity with some object, word, or person rather than from weakness or fault in the moral, spiritual and doctrinal domains--which is where the Bible puts the focus.

D. Territorial Spirits

The doctrine that spirits are connected to certain geographical features (such as caves, mountains, rivers, rocks, etc.) is probably universal in folk religions. And the doctrine that spirits are tied to and exercise their power within certain geographically bounded areas is also common, though not universal. Particularly in contexts where the culturo-political system operates with clear geographical boundaries, one often finds the notion that spirits operate with reference to those boundaries as well. Societies which are nomadic and which operate without reference to political boundaries, on the other hand, seldom stress the notion of spirits as tied to clearly bounded geographical areas.[27] But in many contexts missionaries do find such a

---

[27] In much of Africa and Asia territorial cults were traditionally prevalent, and served cultural functions. But amongst most Amazonian tribal groups, on the other hand, such territorial cults were completely absent, as was the notion of territorial spirits.

notion strongly developed, and many missionaries have been markedly influenced by the idea.

If we examine the appeal to Scripture made by territorial spirits advocates, we find a range of positions. Some casually assert the doctrine to be fully biblical with statements like Dawson's (1991a:xii): "The Bible usually identifies an evil spirit by its territory or its prime characteristic." His lone biblical reference to the "Prince of Persia," however, does not merit the word "usually." More commonly these advocates acknowledge that there is limited biblical teaching on the subject.

Warner tells us that this doctrine is a "familiar concept" among animists, but acknowledges that it "does not seem to be prominent in the New Testament." Yet he forges ahead with his thesis, speculating:

> but depending again on one's world-view, the
> "principalities and powers" of the New Testament
> may well be seen as fitting into this pattern. Our
> cultural "glasses" may make this difficult to bring
> into focus (Warner 1991:137).

That is, Warner suggests, if we could just adjust our cultural "glasses" then we could see that this is what the New Testament is talking about. He makes no effort to exegete the relevant passages. He simply suggests we read such meaning into them. Biblical scholar, Gerry Breshears, is more to the point about the biblical evidence when he says:

> Nowhere in the New Testament do we find a ter-
> ritorial view of demons. Jesus never casts out a
> territorial demon or attributes the resistance of
> Nazareth or Jerusalem to such entities. Paul
> never refers to territorial spirits, nor does he at-
> tribute power to them--despite the paganism of
> the cities where he established churches
> (1994:15).

And what of Warner's notion that the "principalities and powers" of Ephesians be read as territorial spirits? Clinton Arnold, author of **Powers of Darkness** (1992), and **Ephesians: Power and Magic** (1992), responds: "the list of powers in Eph.

6:12, believed by many strategic-warfare advocates to represent territorial spirits, are actually presented as demons that attack individuals" (Arnold 1994:47).

Most of these authors rest the bulk of their argument on other than biblical grounds. Otis, for one, is not daunted by the fact that this doctrine rests on extrabiblical grounds. He offers his response to those who remain unconvinced:

> Those who are frightened away from spiritual territoriality by claims that the concept is extrabiblical should remember that there is an ocean of difference between that which is "extrabiblical" and that which is "unbiblical." Extrabiblical is a yellow light that encourages passage with caution; unbiblical is a red light that requires travelers to halt in the name of the law and common sense. To date, I have heard no one claim that spiritual territoriality is *unbiblical*. The simple reason is that it is not (Otis 1993:35).

But while Otis agrees that the concept is largely extrabiblical, there is one biblical passage, widely taken as implying the existence of territorial spirits, which even the critics of the territorial spirits position have not, until now, subjected to scrutiny. And that is the passage in Daniel 10. All other passages which advocates of spiritual mapping, and spiritual warfare based on that mapping, have appealed to are read in the light of this passage, as well as in the light of anecdotes, native beliefs and demonic revelations. This passage is crucial. If this passage does not teach the notion of demonic territoriality--the notion that demonic power is linked to and exercised over territories--then the other passages fail to persuade. And so we give special attention to this passage.

In Daniel 10 we find Daniel fasting and praying for three weeks. At the end of three weeks, an angel appears to him and tells him that "from the first day" he began praying, his prayer was heard. The angel, coming in response to Daniel's prayer, says "the prince of the kingdom of Persia was withstanding me for twenty-one days," but Michael, "one of the chief princes, came to help me, for I had been left there with the kings of Persia. Now I have come to give you an understanding of what will happen to your people in the latter days" (10:13,14). The angel continues, "I shall now return to fight against the prince of Persia; so I am going forth, and behold, the prince of Greece is about to come" (10:20). Later he refers to another "prince" that will someday defeat a "king of the south" (11:5).

Two issues must be clarified to understand the passage. One issue concerns the identity of the "prince of Persia." Is he a human or a demonic being? The second issue concerns the reason for the twenty-one day delay. Was the angel trying "to get to Daniel" for twenty-one days and couldn't get through? Or was the angel doing battle on behalf of the matter about which Daniel was fasting and praying? The territorial spirits advocates promote one way to understand this passage with little or no consideration given to alternative interpretations. Here are two sample interpretations from the advocates of the notion of territorial spirits:

> In order to get to Daniel, the angel had to battle "the Prince of the kingdom of Persia." The battle lasted twenty-one days and did not finish until the angel Michael came to help him. Then he got through (Wagner 1988a:59).

> On his way from the courts of God to Daniel in Babylon, however, the angel had to pass through the land of Persia. There he was confronted by the guardian angel of Persia, who was so powerful that he held God's messenger at bay for twenty-one days. The messenger angel would never have gotten through with God's answer to Daniel's prayer, except that Michael, the chief archangel, came to his aid. Even now, the angel told Daniel, Michael continued to battle the angel of Persia. The messenger angel concluded, "Now I have to go back and fight the guardian angel of Persia. After that the guardian angel of Greece will appear" (Linthicum 1991:74).

These authors assume that the angel is battling simply to try to win his way through, in a geographical sense, to Daniel. But is this what the passage is saying? Perhaps we should ask, "What is Daniel so concerned about that he would fast and pray for twenty-one days?" The best dating of Daniel 10 indicates that the big issue confronting God's people at that moment was the stoppage of the temple reconstruction. In all likelihood it was this horrifying circumstance about which Daniel was fasting and praying and about which the angel was battling. In verse 13 the angel refers to Michael's assistance in this battle while he (the angel) was "with the kings of Persia." The implication is that the battle somehow concerns the kings of Persia--who of course had political authority over Israel. It was at this time historically that counselors hired by the Samaritans were influencing Persian political leadership against the Jews who were rebuilding the temple (cf. Ezra 4). Both the focus of Daniel's prayer and the focus of the spiritual battle would seem to concern the Jewish people and their rebuilding project as they were adversely affected by action taken by Persian political leadership (Calvin 1948:231-265; Feinberg 1981:142-143; Leupold 1969:456; Shea 1983; Wood 1973:273; Young 1949:224-228; Zimmerman 1970:147-151). God sent the angel to do battle with the being (either human or supernatural) who is somehow accountable for this stoppage, to let Daniel know that his prayer is being addressed, and to communicate other matters of the future.

If we interpret this passage as saying that the angel was trying "to get to" Daniel for twenty-one days and was thwarted, then we must necessarily infer that the "prince" of Persia was a supernatural being.   And since Michael, the archangel, is referred to as a "prince," such an interpretation seems plausible.

But if we interpret this passage as saying that the angel was doing battle with the being responsible for the matter Daniel was fasting and praying about, then we have two options.

First, we may still identify this being as a demon, one influencing government personnel of Persia.   In this case the demon would not be exercising its power through territorial attributes.   That is, the spirit would have been assigned responsibility (by Satan) for the political leadership of Persia, but one could not infer from this that its power was geographical in nature--a "force-field power" linked to a specific geographic expanse, and automatically operative over any being within that territory. Rather the power would be with reference to persons--specifically the king or kings of Persia. On this view, the battle would be between an angel and a demonic being battling over the position of influence with the Persian leadership. This is the interpretation taken by many commentators (see Feinberg

1981:142-143; Leupold   1969:456; Wood   1973:273; Young
1949:224-228; Zimmerman 1970:147-151).

Alternatively, following Calvin (1948), Haevernick
(1832), or William Shea (1983), we may identify the "prince of
Persia" as a human "prince"--the more common usage of the term
in the book of Daniel--who is particularly accountable for what is
occurring. In this third year of the reign of Cyrus, the one who
initially approved the building of the temple, someone put a stop
to the building of the temple. According to cuneiform evidence,
Cyrus appointed his son, Cambyses, King of Babylon--a region
including Israel. Cyrus retained for himself the title of King of
the whole Persian empire. That is, Cambyses had responsibility
for what was happening in Israel, even though Cyrus was still
King. The term "prince," therefore, appropriately fits Cambyses.
Furthermore, the historical record shows that Cambyses, unlike
his father, was known for expressing particular hostility towards
foreign religions (Shea 1983:236-239). According to historical
evidence, then, it is likely that Cambyses was the individual
actively prohibiting the building of the temple, and the individual responsible for the matter Daniel was praying about. On this
interpretation, Cambyses would be the "prince" with whom the
angel was having to contend.[28]

Several observations can now be made. First, even if the
territorial reading of this passage were the correct one (and we
do not believe that it is), there is still an enormous gap between
what can be inferred from this passage and what the advocates
of territorial spirits are teaching. Daniel has no knowledge of
the details of the battle, such as who is fighting whom, or even
knowledge that there is a battle until he is told later. He simply
prays and trusts God for the unseen dimension of things.
Daniel's prayer, therefore, does not depend on any knowledge or
map of such realities on his part, and his prayer is not that of
knowledgeably binding a territorial spirit. It certainly does not
involve binding such a spirit for evangelistic purposes. Therefore, in Daniel 10, the locus classicus for territorial spirits
advocates, even when interpreting the passage as they suggest--
identifying the prince as an evil spirit whose power is exercised
territorially--Daniel does not "discern," "map," "bind," or "pray
against" a territorial spirit.

---

[28] For a fuller exposition of how such an interpretation fits the text and the
historical context, see Calvin (1948:231-266) and Shea (1983).

But many things count against the territorial interpretation of Daniel 10. First, though we cannot fully explore them here, there are hermeneutical and exegetical problems with such an interpretation (cf. Shea 1983). Such problems include the failure 1.) to take into account the historical context, 2.) to take into account the reference in verse 13 to the kings of Persia, and 3.) to adequately account for the reference to the prince of Greece (10:20). Wagner writes:

> The angel told Daniel that on his return trip he not only would have to battle the Prince of Persia but also the Prince of Greece and that again he would only get *through* with Michael's help (1992:66, italics added).

Actually, most commentaries see the reference to the prince of Greece as pointing to a future engagement, a conflict other than that of getting from point A to point B, suggesting that neither should we see the conflict with the prince of Persia as one of simply getting from one point to another. While some commentaries might appear to lend support to the territorial interpretation, on careful inspection most do not. That is, many commentaries will mention that the 21 day delay was due to opposition by a demonic being. But they will often then go on to locate that opposition in terms other than spatial or geographical ones--opposition over influence with Persian kings, for example. Other commentaries fail to make explicit what is understood by that delaying opposition. Many picture the conflict as one which occurs in heaven, perhaps of a legal nature. Others appeal to mystery. We did not find any commentary which fully exposited the text of this chapter (including the reference in verse 13 to the kings of Persia, and the reference in verse 20 to having to return to continue fighting the "prince of Persia") from the consistent vantage point of a territorial reading of this passage. Whatever the correct interpretation of this passage, the current exegetical literature is not solidly behind the territorial reading of the passage.

Furthermore, the idea that territorial spirits exercise dominant control over geographical regions seems to be refuted repeatedly in Scripture. When the Israelites arrived in the promised land they worried that Baal, the god of the land of Canaan, needed to be dealt with. When Naaman was healed, he felt that he should take earth from Israel back to Damascus, so as to worship God on His own soil (II Kgs 5). When Benhadad suffered defeat at the hands of Israel, he inferred that God was a mountain God, so decided to attack next on the plains (I Kgs 20). The Old Testament, however, consistently portrays such notions as false on two grounds. First they are false in assuming that the gods of the nations really did control those regions. Second, they are false in assuming that God had less control in certain regions than in others. During Israel's Babylonian captivity, the Israelites were distressed that they were now distant from the geographical region where their ancestors had worshipped God. They feared that God was not God in this region as well. The overriding message of Isaiah, Ezekiel, Esther and Daniel was that God was equally in control there. "The Most High is sovereign over the kingdoms of men and gives them to anyone He wishes" (Dan 4:25, 32). One is just as close to the courts of heaven in Babylon as in Jerusalem. The notion that an angel sent from heaven to Daniel could have his path blocked for twenty-one days, and then that the angel would have to fight his way back past the territorial spirit to get to the courts of heaven (why else, on this view, is the angel having to return to the fight?) is a notion compatible with animistic thought, but markedly incompatible with biblical thought.

Our final objection to this notion is that it really is but an extension of the first notion that demons can attach to objects and by virtue of a person's physical location *vis a vis* that object, exercise an automatic power over that person. Is a house an object, or a bounded location? It is both. Is the geographic region covered by the Bermuda Triangle or by Uruguay an object or a bounded location? It is both. It is, if you please, a giant object. And if one believes that a simple crossing of the street puts one under the malevolent influence of a spirit (within its "force field"), one is affirming a doctrine exactly comparable to the doctrine that simple contact or ingestion of a physical object like meat is dangerous because it places one under the influence of a demon. This doctrine that spirits can inhabit object or place in such a manner that they throw an aura over it such that physical contiguity by itself gives that demon greater influence or power over an individual than it would otherwise have is a magical/animistic doctrine characteristic of "weaker brothers" rather than of correct doctrinal understanding.

What all these doctrines have in common is the idea that our vulnerability to the power of demons is based on nonmoral and nonspiritual conditions--conditions of physical contiguity and symbolic association with words, objects, persons, and places. The Bible emphasizes that we need to fear Satan's influence in the doctrinal, moral and spiritual arena--that we need to fear sin and deception. These authors, however, tell us that we need to fear Satan's ability to attack based on factors other than our doctrinal, spiritual or moral response. These authors directly invert the biblical emphasis. The Bible calls us to live lives worthy of the God who called us. It assures us that no power on earth can then harm us to stop us from what God calls us to.

CONCLUSION

It is instructive to contrast Paul's approach in I Corinthians with that of these modern missiologists. (i) Paul acknowledges that recent converts from idolatry are mistaken in their notions about the reality and nature of supernatural beings and their powers, and calls them "weaker brothers." These missiologists argue that recent converts from idolatry are in touch with spiritual realities, and they privilege their views. (ii) Paul denies that an object offered to an idol transmits any dangerous influence, even when ingested! These missiologists argue that animists really are correct in believing that spirit power is transmitted by contact with certain physical objects, and that those who doubt it are enlightenment rationalists. (iii) Paul denies the validity of their beliefs, not in the name of naturalism, but of orthodox Christian doctrine. On doctrinal grounds Paul privileges the views of the stronger brothers. These missiologists privilege the views of the weaker brothers, convert to those views, and become vigorous proponents of those views, asking the rest of us to convert as well. (iv) Anthropologically, Paul recognizes that cultural beliefs about such things as idols, spirits, and meat, even though mistaken, do have a reality which must be addressed. That is, he recognizes an independent reality, that of culture. This reality is a reality into which people have been socialized, but it is not a mirror reflection of what actually exists. These authors abandon sound anthropological understanding when they confuse a culture's social construct with reality. Paul is an excellent anthropologist. He does not "go native." But he recognizes that such beliefs have consequences for spiritual life and well-being. And so, unlike the stronger brothers, he is respectful of those with such beliefs and does not ignore such beliefs in his methodology. These authors present two options: either one rejects these beliefs about spirits and is an ineffective missionary, or one embraces such beliefs, fuses one's horizon with that of pagan or recent convert, and has effective ministry and great church growth. Paul rejects both of these options. He rejects the stronger brother insistence that the only consideration is doctrinal. And he rejects the notion of converting doctrinally to the weaker brother position. Instead Paul suggests that we need to take into account the subjective meanings, the culturo-religious meanings of others, and develop pastoral or missiological methods which are sensitive to such subjective cultural realities, but which retain correct doctrinal understandings. This is the route missiology needs to take, but has not yet taken sufficiently. If missiology can recognize that we have started down the wrong path, backtrack, and start down this Pauline path, one which maintains theological integrity in understanding demonic power, anthropological understandings of subjective cultural realities, and methodologies which keep both in view, there is hope for us yet in this difficult area of how to address animists missiologically--whether they be from the Amazon, or from the U.S.A.

REFERENCES CITED

Anderson, Neil T.
> 1990   *The Bondage Breaker.* Eugene, OR: Harvest House Publishers.
> 1991   *The Seduction of our Children.* Eugene, OR: Harvest House Publishers.

Archer, John (compiler)
> 1994   The Devil, Demons & Spiritual Warfare: A Panel of Experts Answer 10 Often-Asked Questions About the Church's Battle Against the Forces of Darkness. *Charisma* 19(7):52-57.

Arnold, Clinton E.
> 1992   *Ephesians: Power and Magic.* Grand Rapids, Mich: Baker Book House.
> 1992   *Powers of Darkness.* Intervarsity Press.
> 1994   What About Territorial Spirits? *Discipleship Journal* 81:47.

Bauman, Harold E.
> 1988   Response to Robert T. Sears. In *Essays on Spiritual Bondage and Deliverance.* (Edited by Willard M. Swartley) Elkhart, Indiana: Institute of Mennonite Studies [Occasional Papers No. 11] 115-117.

Becket, Bob
> 1993   Practical Steps Toward Community Deliverance. In *Breaking Strongholds in Your City: How to Use Spiritual Mapping to Make Your Prayers More Strategic, Effective and Targeted.* (Edited by C. Peter Wagner) Ventura, CA: Regal Books, pp. 147-170.

Bernal, Dick
> 1991   *Curses: What They Are and How to Break Them.* Shippensburg, PA: Companion Press.

Breshears, Gerry
> 1994   The Body of Christ: Prophet, Priest, or King? *Journal of the Evangelical Theological Society* 37 (1):3-26.

Caballeros, Harold
    1993   Defeating the Enemy with the Help of Spiritual
            Mapping. In *Breaking Strongholds in Your City:*
            How to Use Spiritual Mapping to Make Your
            Prayers More Strategic, Effective and Targeted.
            (Edited by C. Peter Wagner) Ventura, CA: Regal
            Books, pp. 123-145.

Calvin, John
    1948   *Commentaries on the Book of the Prophet Daniel.*
            (Trans. by Thomas Myers). Grand Rapids:
            Eerdmans.

Chiundiza, Richmond
    1991   High Level Powers in Zimbabwe. In *Engaging*
            the Enemy: How to Fight and Defeat Territorial
            Spirits. (Edited by C. Peter Wagner) Ventura,
            CA: Regal Books, pp. 121-127.

Dawson, John
    1989   *Taking Our Cities for God: How to Break*
            Spiritual Strongholds. Lake Mary, FL: Creation
            House
    1991a   Foreword. In *Engaging the Enemy: How to Fight*
            and Defeat Territorial Spirits. (Edited by C.
            Peter Wagner) Ventura, CA: Regal Books, pp. ix-
            xvi.
    1991b   Seventh Time Around: Breaking Through a City's
            Invisible Barriers to the Gospel. In *Engaging the*
            Enemy: How to Fight and Defeat Territorial
            Spirits. (Edited by C. Peter Wagner) Ventura,
            CA: Regal Books, pp. 135-142.

Dickason, C. Fred
    1987   *Demon Possession and the Christian.* Chicago:
            Moody Press.

Erickson, Millard J.
    1993   *Evangelical Mind and Heart: Perspectives on*
            Theological and Practical Issues. Grand Rapids:
            Baker Book House.

Eysenck, H. J.
    1993   Forty Years On: The Outcome Problem in
            Psychotherapy Revisited. In *Handbook of*
            Effective Psychotherapy. (Ed. by Thomas R.
            Giles) New York: Plenum Press, 3-20.

Feinberg, Charles Lee
>   1981   *Daniel: The Man and His Visions.* Chappaqua,
>   New York: Christian Herald Books.
Gailey, Charles R.
>   1994   Review of "Engaging the Enemy: How to Fight
>   and Defeat Territorial Spirits." *Missiology*
>   22:250.
Garrett, Susan R.
>   1989   *The Demise of the Devil: Magic and the Demonic
>   in Luke's Writings.* Minneapolis: Fortress Press.
Geisler, Norman
>   1988   *Signs and Wonders.* Wheaton: Tyndale House.
Greenlee, David
>   1994   Territorial Spirits Reconsidered. *Missiology*
>   22:507-514.
Haevernick, H. C.
>   1832   *Commentar ueber das Buch Daniel.*
Harper, Michael
>   1984   *Spiritual Warfare.* Ann Arbor, Mich: Servant
>   Books.
Hiebert, Paul G.
>   1982   The Flaw of the Excluded Middle. *Missiology*
>   10:35-47.
>   1989   Healing and the Kingdom. *Wonders and the
>   Word: An Examination of Issues Raised by John
>   Wimber and the Vineyard Movement.* (Edited by
>   James R. Coggins and Paul G. Hiebert) Hillsboro,
>   KS: Kindred Press, pp. 109-152.
>   1992   Biblical Perspectives on Spiritual Warfare.
>   *Mission Focus* 20(3):41-50.
Hummel, Charles E.
>   1993   *Fire in the Fireplace: Charismatic Renewal in the
>   Nineties.* Downers Grove, Ill: InterVarsity Press.
Intercession Working Group of the Lausanne Committee for
World Evangelization
>   1995   Excerpts from the Statement on Spiritual
>   Warfare. *Evangelical Missions Quarterly 31156-
>   157.*
Jacobs, Cindy
>   1991   *Possessing the Gates of the Enemy.* Grand
>   Rapids, Mich: Chosen Books.

1993 Dealing With Strongholds. In *Breaking Strongholds in Your City: How to Use Spiritual Mapping to Make Your Prayers More Strategic, Effective and Targeted.* (Edited by C. Peter Wagner) Ventura, CA: Regal Books, pp. 73-95.

Kole, Andre and Al Janssen
 1984 *Miracles or Magic?* Grand Rapids: Harvest House.

Kraft, Charles
 1989 *Christianity with Power: Your Worldview and Your Experience of the Supernatural.* Ann Arbor, Mich: Servant Publications.
 1992 *Defeating Dark Angels: Breaking Demonic Oppression in the Believer's Life.* Ann Arbor, Mich: Servant Publications.
 1993 *Deep Wounds Deep Healing: Discovering the Vital Link Between Spiritual Warfare and Inner Healing.* Ann Arbor, Michigan: Servant Publications.
 1994a Dealing with Demonization. In *Behind Enemy Lines: An Advanced Guide to Spiritual Warfare.* (Edited by Charles Kraft and Mark White) Ann Arbor, Michigan: Servant Publications, pp. 79-120.
 1994b Spiritual Power: Principles and Observations. In *Behind Enemy Lines: An Advanced Guide to Spiritual Warfare.* (Edited by Charles Kraft and Mark White) Ann Arbor, Michigan: Servant Publications, pp. 31-62.
 1994c Two Kingdoms in Conflict. In *Behind Enemy Lines: An Advanced Guide to Spiritual Warfare.* (Edited by Charles Kraft and Mark White) Ann Arbor, Michigan: Servant Publications, pp. 17-29.

Kusche, Lawrence
 1975 *The Bermuda Triangle Mystery--Solved.* New York: Harper and Row.
 1980 *The Disappearance of Flight 19.* New York: Harper and Row.

Lawson, Steven
 1991 Defeating Territorial Spirits. In *Engaging the Enemy: How to Fight and Defeat Territorial*

Spirits. (Edited by C. Peter Wagner) Ventura, CA: Regal Books, pp. 29-41.

Lea, Larry
    1991   Binding the Strongman. In *Engaging the Enemy: How to Fight and Defeat Territorial Spirits.* (Edited by C. Peter Wagner) Ventura, CA: Regal Books, pp. 83-95.

Leupold, H. G.
    1969   *Exposition of Daniel.* Grand Rapids, Michigan: Baker Book House.

Linthicum, Robert C.
    1991   *City of God, City of Satan: A Biblical Theology of the Urban Church.* Grand Rapids, Mich: Zondervan Publishing House.

Loewen, Jacob
    1991   Which God do Missionaries Preach? In *Engaging the Enemy: How to Fight and Defeat Territorial Spirits.* (Edited by C. Peter Wagner) Ventura, CA: Regal Books, pp. 165-175.

Long, Paul B.
    1991   Don't Underestimate the Opposition. In *Engaging the Enemy: How to Fight and Defeat Territorial Spirits.* (Edited by C. Peter Wagner) Ventura, CA: Regal Books, pp. 129-133.

Lorenzo, Victor
    1993   Evangelizing a City Dedicated to Darkness. In *Breaking Strongholds in Your City: How to Use Spiritual Mapping to Make Your Prayers More Strategic, Effective and Targeted.* (Edited by C. Peter Wagner) Ventura, CA: Regal Books, pp. 171-193.

MacNutt, Francis and Judith MacNutt
    1988   *Praying for Your Unborn Child.* New York: Doubleday.

Martin, Dennis
    1988   Resisting the Devil in the Patristic, Medieval, and Reformation Church. In *Essays on Spiritual Bondage and Deliverance.* (Edited by Willard M. Swartley) Elkhart, Indiana: Institute of Mennonite Studies [Occasional Papers No. 11] 46-71.

McAll, Kenneth
    1991   *Healing the Family Tree.* London: Sheldon Press.
McGregor, Mark and Bev Klopp
    1993   Mapping and Discerning Seattle, Washington. In
            *Breaking Strongholds in Your City: How to Use
            Spiritual Mapping to Make Your Prayers More
            Strategic, Effective and Targeted.* (Edited by C.
            Peter Wagner) Ventura, CA: Regal Books, pp.
            197-222.
Moreau, A. Scott
    1995   Religious Borrowing as a Two-Way Street: An
            Introduction to Animistic Tendencies in the Euro-
            North American Context. In *Christianity and the
            Religions.* Edited by Edward Rommen and
            Harold Netland. Pasadena: William Carey
            Library, pp. 166-182.
Murphy, Ed
    1992   *Handbook for Spiritual Warfare.* Nashville:
            Thomas Nelson Publishers.
Otis, George
    1991   *The Last of the Giants.* Tarrytown, New York:
            Chosen Books.
    1993   An Overview of Spiritual Mapping. In *Breaking
            Strongholds in Your City: How to Use Spiritual
            Mapping to Make Your Prayers More Strategic,
            Effective and Targeted.* (Edited by C. Peter
            Wagner) Ventura, CA: Regal Books, pp. 29-47.
Page, Sydney H.T.
    1995   *Powers of Evil: A Biblical Study of Satan and
            Demons.* Grand Rapids: Baker Book House.
Powlison, David
    1995   *Power Encounters: Reclaiming Spiritual Warfare.*
            Grand Rapids, Michigan: Baker Books.
Priest, Robert J.
    1993   *Defilement, Moral Purity, and Transgressive
            Power: The Symbolism of Filth in Aguaruna
            Jivaro Culture.* Berkeley, CA: University of
            California, PhD Dissertation.
Prince, Derek
    1986   *From Curse to Blessing.* Ft. Lauderdale, FL:
            Derek Prince Ministries.

1990   *Blessing or Curse: You Can Choose.* Old Tappan, N.J.: Chosen Books.

Robb, John
1993   Satan's Tactics in Building and Maintaining His Kingdom of Darkness. *International Journal of Frontier Missions* 10(4): 173-184.

1994   How Satan Works at the Cosmic Level. In *Behind Enemy Lines: An Advanced Guide to Spiritual Warfare.* (Edited by Charles Kraft and Mark White) Ann Arbor, Michigan: Servant Publications, pp. 165-197.

Sears, Robert T., S.J.
1988   A Catholic View of Exorcism and Deliverance. In *Essays on Spiritual Bondage and Deliverance.* (Edited by Willard M. Swartley) Elkhart, Indiana: Institute of Mennonite Studies [Occasional Paper No. 11] 100-114.

Shea, William H.
1983   Wrestling with the Prince of Persia: A Study on Daniel 10. *Andrews University Seminary Studies* 21(3):225-250.

Shibley, David
1989   *A Force in the Earth: The Charismatic Renewal and World Evangelism.* Altamonte Springs, FL: Creation House.

Silvoso, Edgardo
1991   Prayer Power in Argentina. In *Engaging the Enemy: How to Fight and Defeat Territorial Spirits.* (Edited by C. Peter Wagner) Ventura, CA: Regal Books, pp. 109-115.

Sjöberg, Kjell
1993   Spiritual Mapping for Prophetic Prayer Actions. In *Breaking Strongholds in Your City: How to Use Spiritual Mapping to Make Your Prayers More Strategic, Effective and Targeted.* (Edited by C. Peter Wagner) Ventura, CA: Regal Books, pp. 97-119.

Sterk, Vernon
1991   Territorial Spirits and Evangelization in Hostile Environments. In *Engaging the Enemy: How to Fight and Defeat Territorial Spirits.* (Edited by

C. Peter Wagner) Ventura, CA: Regal Books, pp. 145-163.

Sumrall, Lester F.
1954 *Modern Manila Miracles.* Springfield, MO: Clifton O. Erickson.
1955 *The True Story of Clarita Villanueva: A Seventeen-year-old Girl Bitten by Devils in Bilibid Prison.* Manila, Philippines.
1986 Deliverance: Setting the Captives Free. *World Harvest* (July/August 1986):6-7.

Tuggy, A. Leonard and Ralph Toliver
1972 *Seeing the Church in the Philippines.* Manila: OMF Publishers.

Vitz, Paul C.
1992 Leaving Psychology Behind. In *No God but God.* (Edited by Os Guinness and John Seef) Chicago: Moody Press, pp. 95-110.

Wagner, C. Peter
1985 Can Demons Harm Christians? *Christian Life* 47(1):76.
1988a *How to Have a Healing Ministry Without Making Your Church Sick.* Ventura, CA: Regal Books.
1988b *The Third Wave of the Holy Spirit.* Ann Arbor, Michigan: Servant Publications.
1989 Territorial Spirits and World Mission. *Evangelical Missions Quarterly* 25:278-288.
1990 Territorial Spirits. In *Wrestling With Dark Angels: Toward a Deeper Understanding of the Supernatural Forces in Spiritual Warfare.* (Edited by C. Peter Wagner and F. Douglas Pennoyer). Ventura, CA: Regal Books, pp. 73-99.
1991a Spiritual Warfare. In *Engaging the Enemy: How to Fight and Defeat Territorial Spirits.* (Edited by C. Peter Wagner) Ventura, CA: Regal Books, pp. 3-27.
1991b Territorial Spirits. In *Engaging the Enemy: How to Fight and Defeat Territorial Spirits.* (Edited by C. Peter Wagner) Ventura, CA: Regal Books, pp. 43-54.
1992 *Warfare Prayer.* Ventura, CA: Regal Books.
1993a Introduction. In *Breaking Strongholds in Your City: How to Use Spiritual Mapping to Make*

Your Prayers More Strategic, Effective and Targeted. (Edited by C. Peter Wagner) Ventura, CA: Regal Books, pp. 11-26.

1993b   Summary: Mapping Your Community. In *Breaking Strongholds in Your City: How to Use Spiritual Mapping to Make Your Prayers More Strategic, Effective and Targeted.* (Edited by C. Peter Wagner) Ventura, CA: Regal Books, pp. 223-232.

1993c   The Visible and the Invisible. In *Breaking Strongholds in Your City: How to Use Spiritual Mapping to Make Your Prayers More Strategic, Effective and Targeted.* (Edited by C. Peter Wagner) Ventura, CA: Regal Books, pp. 49-72.

1994   *Spreading the Fire.* Ventura, CA: Regal Books.

1995   *Lighting the World: A New Look At Acts--God's Handbook for World Evangelism.* (The Acts of the Holy Spirit Series: Book 2). Ventura, CA: Regal Books.

Wagner, C. Peter (ed.)

1991   *Engaging the Enemy: How to Fight and Defeat Territorial Spirits.* Ventura, CA: Regal Books.

1993   *Breaking Strongholds in Your City: How to Use Spiritual Mapping to Make Your Prayers More Strategic, Effective and Targeted.* Ventura, CA: Regal Books.

Wakely, Mike

1995   A Critical Look at a new "Key" to evangelization. *Evangelical Missions Quarterly* 31:152-162.

Warner, Timothy M.

1986   Power Encounter with the Demonic. In *Evangelism on the Cutting Edge.* (Edited by Robert E. Coleman) Old Tappan, New Jersey: Fleming H. Revell Company, pp. 89-101.

1991a   Dealing With Territorial Demons. In *Engaging the Enemy: How to Fight and Defeat Territorial Spirits.* (Edited by C. Peter Wagner) Ventura, CA: Regal Books, pp. 51-54.

1991b   *Spiritual Warfare: Victory Over the Powers of This Dark World.* Wheaton: Crossway Books.

1994   Satan Hates You and Has a Terrible Plan for Your Life. *Discipleship Journal* 81:26-31.

White, Thomas B.
 1990   *The Believer's Guide to Spiritual Warfare.* Ann
         Arbor: Vine.
 1991   Understanding Principalities and Powers. In
         *Engaging the Enemy: How to Fight and Defeat
         Territorial Spirits.* (Edited by C. Peter Wagner)
         Ventura, CA: Regal Books, pp. 59-67.
 1993   *Breaking Strongholds: How Spiritual Warfare
         Sets Captive Free.* Ann Arbor, Michigan: Servant
         Publications.
 1994   Is This Really Warfare? *Discipleship Journal*
         81:33-37.
Wood, Leon
 1973   *A Commentary on Daniel.* Grand Rapids:
         Zondervan.
Yamamori, Ted and George Otis, Jr.
 1992   The Vital Role of the Spiritual Mapping Track.
         Mission Frontiers 14 (1-3):15.
Young, Edward J.
 1949   *The Prophecy of Daniel: A Commentary.* Grand
         Rapids: William B. Eerdmans.
Zimmerman, Felix H.
 1970   *Daniel in Babylon.* Broadview, Illinois: Gibbs
         Publishing Company.

2

"CHRISTIAN ANIMISM" OR GOD-GIVEN AUTHORITY?

Charles H. Kraft[1]

INTRODUCTION

The chapter by Priest, Cambell and Mullen to which I am replying leaves me incredulous and makes this a very difficult chapter to write. It is hard for me to believe that someone with anthropological credentials (Priest) could so completely miss the crucial differences between animism and the use of God-given authority that it is our privilege as Christians to participate in (see Mt 10:1; Lk 9:1; Jn 14:12). These authors apparently cannot tell the difference between the position we have in Christ that authorizes us to use His authority to convey His power, and the animistic assumption that power automatically inheres in certain objects and places.

So, for reasons probably unconscious to them, they have turned what could and should have been a reasoned, scholarly airing by people who trust each other, though holding different views on an important subject, into a diatribe against certain views that they insist on referring to pejoratively as "animist" and "magical." This they do in spite of the fact that *their definitions of these concepts in no way apply to the clear statements I and most of the rest of us who were attacked have made concerning what we believe and practice.* I am not denying the danger that some who imitate us might unwittingly fall into animistic understandings of spiritual power. After all, these "expert" authors have made such a mistake in interpretation if not in practice. But to accuse those they cite of making this mistake is very wide of the mark. What little

---

[1] Charles Kraft teaches at Fuller Seminary.

sense the charge that we are into animism ever made (e.g. in the original paper) disappeared as soon as they defined what they meant by the term animism. I am sad, therefore, as I respond, not because they have challenged us but because of the tone of their piece. We who are attacked are put on the defensive and are treated as enemies rather than fellow-missiologists who seek to deal with problems that are very real to missionaries.

But, though their charges are frivolous, as I hope to demonstrate below, I am glad that the issues they raised (and others) concerning spiritual power will now be discussed openly by concerned evangelical missiologists. For if we are to learn what we would like to learn in this area, we need open discussion of the issues. We who practice and write in this area and have chosen to let others see and evaluate our perspectives also need to come to grips with others' perceptions of what we are into. Perhaps there are places where we have mis- or overstated our case or given the impression that theories that we are testing and experiments we are conducting are more solid than they really are. In spite, then, of the nature of the stimulus, I will try my best to reply in a way that is as helpful as possible to you, the audience.

For a start, I want to state that I believe we can expect the kinds of regularity in the spirit realm that scientists have found in their studies of the physical and human worlds (see Kraft 1994). My quest, then, beyond my desire to see people set free from satanic interference in their lives, is to seek to discover the principles and regularities that obtain in the relationships between the spirit world and the human world. As with the development of the physical and the social sciences, the development of a science that concerns itself with spiritual reality will require a good bit of interaction between those with differing points of view. We will inevitably find that there are differences of opinion based on differences in perspective. Such differences in perspective, then, are influenced by many things, including differences in background, differences in understandings, differences in experience and differences in willingness to risk. The paper that initiated this discussion manifests all of these differences and perhaps more, plus distrust engendered by the fear that those for whom I speak will mislead missionaries, missiologists and others into animism.

In spite of such differences and the sharpness of the original article, I welcome this opportunity to represent our side in this discussion. I propose to do so as best I can by first dealing with several of the issues I consider basic and then by attempting to answer whatever remain of the more substantial of the accusations leveled at us.

AN APOLOGY

I think the best place to start is with an apology for the times when we on my side of these issues have overstated our cases, exaggerated our claims and used poor sources for our anecdotes. I will be more careful myself and recommend more care to my colleagues based on this serious misreading of our approach. As I apologize, though, and as I attempt to deal with the issues at hand, I can only speak confidently from my own perspective (though I will try at many points to accurately represent at least some of the others).

We have, however, as charged, been sloppy at times with the illustrations we have used. And we have, at times, given the impression that what we are experimenting with is more solidly established than it really is. For example, though I have not spoken to Wagner about it, I believe he would join me in regretting the places where he, others and Sumrall himself have misstated and/or misinterpreted the illustration presented on pp 46-48 of the Priest, Campbell and Mullen chapter. Nor can we accept McCall's (1991) interpretation of what caused the Bermuda Triangle problem (see below), even though many of us believe there is data there that needs to be interpreted from a supernaturalistic rather than a naturalistic perspective.

Further, I regret any implication that feelings alone establish the presence of demonic beings and influence. Neither I nor the others for whom I speak are so naive as to believe that such feelings are dependable in and of themselves (see below), even though we believe that certain people are spiritually gifted with greater sensitivity in this area than others and, therefore, should be taken seriously when they claim to feel something.

In addition, we may on occasion be guilty of the overenthusiasm of those who have been discovering new things. I believe we have indeed been discovering new things (not inventing new doctrines)--things that should be taken seriously by all of us. But, as with all such discovery, it is easy to overstate and to credit experiments and theories with greater factuality than they warrant. I apologize for this for myself and, if they will permit me, for the others on my side of the fence built by our critics.

I also apologize here at the start for the defensive tone of some of what follows. I have tried to be unemotional about it but have found no gentle way to make some of the points I wish to make to counter the harshness of some of our critics' attacks. We are accused of corrupting the missiological community. This is not a charge to be taken lightly and I know of no way to answer it, and the detailed way the charge is developed, except to take the issues "to the mat."

At this point, I'd like to point out something that is probably not obvious from the chapter by Priest, Campbell and Mullen: In spite of their attempt to lump us all together and to condemn us *en masse*, we who are attacked by them are not all in the same place on every issue. We have some differences of perspective, some differences of experience and some differences of interpretation, not to mention some differences in the way we handle data and in the risks we are willing to take in presenting our theories. Though, for example, I have gotten much reliable information from demons under pressure from the Holy Spirit (see below), I would not go as far as they quote Murphy as going in asserting the truthfulness of the kinds of information they give that cannot be checked. Likewise, we all, including Rita Cabezas de Krumm (1992) herself, are very careful to regard the information she received concerning the demonic hierarchy (pp 28-29) as extremely tentative at best, though worthy of presenting for others to react to. It is interesting that our critics regard Wagner's tentativeness as "curious" (p 29), probably because they have already made up their minds that he is gullible. Anyway, where our willingness to share our data, even "far out" data such as this, for others to react to has led even those readers who are open to draw wrong conclusions either about the data or about our certainty, I apologize.

All of us who are criticized share with Priest, Campbell and Mullen a commitment to Christ, to the authority of the Scriptures and to the task of world evangelization. If we have given any other impression, I apologize. In addition, most of us share with these critics an evangelical, non-charismatic background. We know, though, that experience strongly affects our interpretations of the Bible (see below) and that there is more in the Scriptures than most of us have yet mined, especially with regard to the spirit world. We, therefore, seek to present our experiences with our attempts to interpret them and their relationship to the Scriptures with full recognition that 1) new understandings may be threatening, especially to the more conservative and less experienced (in the area under investigation) and 2) that there may be greater insight for all of us if we are venturesome, risking in faith in God to perhaps discover some of that additional truth that He promised us (Jn 16:13).

A CRUCIAL MISSIOLOGICAL ISSUE

Missiology has to deal with a plethora of spirit-world problems that have not been adequately dealt with in the past. We need, then, to come up with theories concerning these problems and to test them in practice. A number of the points our critics raise should, therefore, be discussed in an open, trusting manner in which we sift experience (not just theory) in the light of what we think Scripture means and vice-versa. This should be a top missiological agenda item.

I have already suggested that I believe the biggest problem in worldwide Christianity is what I call "dual allegiance" (see Kraft and Kraft 1993). With this term I label the kind of situation in which Christians, though they have committed themselves to Christ, continue to go to shamans, diviners and the like to meet their felt need for spiritual power. The gospel message has encountered them at the point of allegiance and they study the Scriptures to discover God's truths but they have not come to experience anything within Christianity that confronts and replaces their previous sources of spiritual power (see Kraft 1991). In spite of the prominence of the exercise of God's power through humans, it is an unfortunate fact that Christians all over the world are practicing a Christianity devoid of the ability to deal with the spirit world. Or they go about trying to deal with it in really strange ways. There are, of course, historical reasons for this, most of which have to do with deficiencies in the worldviews of the western advocates of Christianity.

Fortunately, many western missiologists are beginning to recognize these deficiencies and to try to do something about them. No longer do we ignore or simply condemn the concern for power among nonwestern (or even western) peoples. In an attitude of repentance over the ignorance that led many of us to ignore or mislead those we worked with, some of us are seeking to learn and teach in this area. For, we feel, if the Christianity of missionized areas, not to mention that of Euroamerica, is to be properly biblical, issues of spiritual power need to be on the front burner of missiological investigation. We evangelicals have ignored them for too long.

As we explore matters pertaining to the spirit world, we are attempting to pioneer in an area heretofore virtually unexplored by evangelicals and long ignored by missiologists. We do so with a desire to learn as well as to share what God has been teaching us. We want to work carefully and wisely in this area so that what we come up with will be biblical, balanced and helpful both at home and abroad. We agree, then, with Priest, Campbell and Mullen that the issues they raised are important. They are, in fact, issues we are actively trying to sort out ourselves. Such discussion is cutting-edge missiology and requires the best we can give it.

Unfortunately, the authors of the preceding chapter seem to have been unduly influenced by their fears. They fear that our writings and teaching will make people insecure. They fear that we will lead people into heresy. They fear that missionaries will change their strategies from what they are now doing (which, by the way, is often not working) to something we might suggest. They fear that we will have to admit that animists understand some things about the spirit world better than we do. They fear that there might be some truth about the spirit world outside of their paradigm. They fear to trust the experiences even of other evangelical Christians (like us) who have gone farther into these areas than they have. And they fear the interpretations of Scripture of these other Christians, lest they be too influenced by experiences they do not understand. None of these fears, of course, prove that our positions are correct. But they form a very flimsy foundation from which to launch the kind of attack Priest and colleagues have launched.

The issue of what to do about spiritual power was once at the heart of the way westerners understood our mission to the nonwestern world. Missionaries and missiologists of a century ago understood that the essence of mission was the confrontation between God and Satan. Unfortunately, mission practice was usually built on the assumption that God had so influenced western cultures and Satan so influenced "pagan" cultures that the encounter between God and Satan involved the stamping out of their Satan-infected way of life, replacing it with our "God-ordained" customs. To bring this about, we introduced western schools, churches and medicine as if these were the God-ordained instruments for Christianizing the nonChristian world.

In reaction, along came a generation of missionaries and missiologists (myself included) who focused on appreciating, accepting and using culture for the sake of the gospel. We began to understand and teach that nonwestern cultures are not totally bad, while western cultures are not totally good. And every culture is usable by God for His purposes. In our optimism about culture, however, we tended to pay too little attention to the fact that Satan also uses culture precipitating the kind of spiritual warfare we see throughout the nonChristian world as well as throughout the Bible. Though we encountered people at the point of their need to commit themselves to Christ and pointed them to the truths of Scripture and Christian experience, we evangelicals had nothing to offer them either to confront or to replace their sources of spiritual power (see Kraft 1991). We thus grew a powerless Christianity, much like ours at home. And large numbers of nonwestern Christians to this day follow a powerless Christ and go to native priests, diviners, shamans and medical practitioners when they need healing or supernatural guidance (see Kraft & Kraft 1993).

We had learned that culture is not the enemy but didn't know what to do about the one who is the enemy and who operates in every cultural context. Into this void for me (and Wagner) came a credible witness named John Wimber--an evangelical whom God had led into a calm but powerful healing ministry. He taught us, by word and demonstration, what God had been teaching him concerning the authority Jesus gave believers to minister in the power of the Holy Spirit (Lk 9:1; Jn 14:12; Mt 28:19-20; Ac 1:8). He also taught us that the Great Commission, like Jesus' life and ministry, has two parts to it: a "proclaim" part and a "heal" part (Lk 9:2). And we began to learn that Jesus is keeping His promise that we who have faith in Him have the authority to do what He did while He was on earth (Jn 14:12).

We began to see and participate in healings and deliverances in abundance happening as we operated in the authority Jesus gave us to claim the power of God for healing and deliverance. We also began to listen to God more and to experience what are often called "words of knowledge" (1 Cor 12:8)--insight given by God to assist in ministry. This ability is not, as our authors contend, a "spiritual geiger counter," but a way that God has used throughout history (and Scripture) to reveal things to humans. In this way both OT and NT servants of God regularly received guidance from Him. For example, it was via word of knowledge that the disciples heard from the Holy Spirit that they should choose Barnabas and Saul "to do the work to which I have called them" (Ac 13:2). This was also the way Jesus got insight since, in obedience to the Father, He did not use His divine attributes (including His omniscience) while on earth. Had He retained His omniscience, He could not have claimed not to know concerning the end times in Mark 13:32.

Though it is difficult to speak of the profoundness of the paradigm and practice shifts (see Kraft 1989) we have undergone without seeming self-serving, I will risk it. For this will be a major factor at several points in our discussion where there are differences of interpretation of Scripture and life experience. Not that these shifts make our understandings more correct than those of our critics. These shifts, though, mean that we often see different things when looking at the same data. My paradigm and practice shifts, and the equivalents for other members of the group being criticized, have profoundly changed our lives and our approach to ministry and missiology. For myself, after 38 years (1944-1982) of solid evangelical Christian experience, the Bible has become in the last 13 years a new book, a book with a much deeper spiritual level than I had ever seen before. I have found myself experientially much closer to the New Testament since I have been participating with God in releasing prisoners from captivity as Jesus did. This has brought into our lives a body of experience that colors our interpretations of life and the Scriptures. It is incredibly moving to be experiencing daily the kinds of things we read about in the Gospels (e.g. hearing things from God that prove out, as well as healings and deliverances) and to be discovering in practice that Jesus has kept His promise that "whoever believes in me will do what I do" (Jn 14:12). It is also incredibly humbling to be constantly involved in doing and experiencing things (e.g. healings and deliverances) that we know we can't do unless the Holy Spirit is present to make them happen.

Priest, Campbell and Mullen claim they are not "enlightenment rationalists who refuse to accept the validity of any account of the supernatural" (p 25). Their statement is almost believable with respect to their perspective but not with respect to their practice. They seem to stand barely on the supernaturalistic side of the paradigm shift into supernaturalism but with a long way to go to get to the crucial shift, what I have called the "practice shift." There is nothing wrong with being where they are as long as they don't either misjudge what they can understand from there or dig in and move no farther. They say then that they are "biblicists who refuse uncritically to trust reported experiences of the supernatural which advance 'new doctrine'" (p 25). Good. So are we, though we may at times be more credulous than we intend to be. But we work from farther along the scale because we have been able to add the practice dimension to the perspective from which we interpret, and to the vantage point from which we test new ideas. From this position many things look biblical to us that do not to them because they seem to fit with a degree of biblical supernaturalism they cannot yet see. Thus, much of what they from their perspective see as "new doctrine" is to us both scripturally and experientially valid. "Biblicism" looks different from either side of the practice shift.

They decry the coming into existence of what they call "new doctrinal understandings of demonic power--derived from paradigm-shift experiences" (p 10). They even suggest that the fact that we talk to demons means that some of these doctrines come from demons (cf 1 Tim 4:1). These are weighty charges and I will get to them below. But if there is further truth out there (Jn 16:13), and I believe there is, we need to risk going beyond our old understandings. Inevitably, though, the more conservative and less experienced among us will perceive any departure from, or going beyond, their pre-paradigm-shift assumptions as a threat to their system. Again, as I have contended above, we need a more sober discussion of these ideas in a context (unlike this one) of mutual trust and at least some sharing of experience in the realm of the spiritual realities we are discussing. In such discussion, though, we need to refrain from frivolous accusations such as that we are advocating doctrines of demons.

As for "new doctrinal understandings," is not their naturalistic interpretation of Daniel 10 a new doctrine? Or their refusal to allow Satan any but a nominal role in human life in spite of the position the NT gives him (e.g. "ruler" [Jn 14:30; Eph 2:2], "evil god of this world" [2 Cor 4:4])? Or their denial of the efficacy of curses and blessings? Are our interpretations "new doctrines," while theirs, no matter how naturalistic and/or fanciful, and no matter how incongruent with much experience (which, unfortunately, they have not shared in) are to be taken as normative? These authors say they are open to proposals of new understandings (p 41). It will, I'm afraid, take a considerable change of stance to prove this.

The fact that our critics are mistaken with these criticisms does not make us necessarily right and them wrong. The recognition that we approach our topic from opposite sides of a paradigm shift does, however, explain how both they and we can claim to be biblical, yet differ so widely at points. It especially helps explain how they can be so wide of the mark in their misunderstanding of the differences between animism and the employment of biblical authority and power (see below).

AUTHORITY

I would now like to say a few words about authority. Jesus said that He is sending us, just as the Father sent Him (Jn 20:21). And He said He came powerless (Jn 5:19), having in some mysterious way put aside His Divine knowledge, power and other prerogatives (Phil 2:6-8). He worked, therefore, in total dependence on the Father. Thus, He was able to do no mighty works before the Holy Spirit came upon Him at His baptism. But then, full of the Holy Spirit and obedient to and dependent on the Father, He did His works as a human being empowered by the Holy Spirit. When Jesus left, then, He promised the same Holy Spirit to His followers (Ac 1:4-5) to enable us to do the same and greater works than He did (Jn 14:12). As with Jesus, then, the Holy Spirit is our Source of power and Jesus Himself our Authority-giver and our Model.

The thing that startled people in Jesus' ministry was the fact that He spoke (Mt 7:29) and cast out demons (Mk 1:27) with *authority*. During His ministry, Jesus gave that authority to His disciples along with the power of the Holy Spirit (Mt 10:1; Lk 9:1). When He left the earth, then, He instructed His followers to teach their followers all that He had taught them, presumably including how to minister in that power and authority (Mt 28:20; Lk 24:49; Ac 1:4, 8). Earlier He had told them that whoever has faith in Him would have the authority to do His works (Jn 14:12).

It is as if Jesus came to earth with a credit card with God the Father's name at the top and Jesus' name under it (as I did with one of my sons when he was in college). This meant that Jesus had all the authority that the *Father's* name would bring. When Jesus left, then, he passed the credit card on to His followers, including us, with His name at the top and ours under it. In doing so, He gave us the authority to use His name to bring about His will (Jn 14:13-14). So we have the authority to regularly use the formula, "In Jesus' name" to convey the power of God, not automatically as in magic, but out of our relationship with Jesus and the authority that relationship gives us.

The difference between working under the authority of God and magic is crucial to this discussion. With magic, the use of formulas and rituals is believed to automatically bring about the desired result. If, then, the process doesn't work, the conclusion is that a mistake has been made in the procedure. Though in actuality, it is Satan that works behind the scenes to empower or not empower the formulas, he deceives people into thinking they are in control through correct use of the formulas and rituals. Beyond magic, then, animist priests often believe they can control spirits to do their bidding when, in actuality, it is they who are being used by the spirits.

Working under the authority of God, as servants of Christ are privileged to do, is quite another thing. We do not control God. We submit to Him, following Jesus' example. As Jesus modeled life under the direction of the Father, it is our first job to listen to God, then to do what we hear from Him as Jesus did (Jn 8:28; cf Jn 5:19, 30). When we do this, finding His will and conforming to that will (as best we understand it) our use of the authority given us, Jesus assures us that He will do what we ask (Jn 14:13-14). This is the proper exercise of the authority that has been graciously given to us by God. When formulas are used (e.g. "in Jesus' name), therefore, the results flow from the relationship and the obedience to the personal Source of power behind the formula, not from the formula itself. This is what we do and teach. Our critics seem not to understand this crucial point.

The sons of Sceva tried to use Jesus' name, but without the authority given by the relationship with Jesus. And they got exposed and beaten for their attempt to use an authority that was not theirs (Ac 19:11-16). We need fear no such outcome as long as we keep on good terms with Jesus, the source of our authority. It is an awesome thing to experience a demon's response both to the authority of Jesus and to the knowledge that we have a right to work in that authority. On several occasions I have seen the whole demeanor of a demon change in response to the question, "Do you recognize that I come in the name of Jesus Christ?" Their arrogance fades, their tone of voice betrays submission and sometimes the demonized person experiences their trembling in the presence of one who represents the Lord to whom the demons will one day be forced to bow their knees and "proclaim that Jesus Christ is Lord, to the glory of God the Father" (Phil 2:11).

ANIMISM AND MAGIC

At this point it will help to examine animism and magic. On pages 13-14 of their chapter, Priest and his colleagues make explicit what they mean by magic and link animism to it. As a matter of fact, animism is much broader than they indicate, involving a rather wide range of principles and practices relating to the spirit world. Since there is a true set of principles and practices that God Himself has put in the universe on the basis of which humans are to relate to the spirit world (see Kraft 1994:31-62), and since animists are not as ignorant as our authors make them out to be (see below), and since they specialize in dealing with the spirit world, we can expect that animists have discovered at least some of these principles. *The ways in which animists misanalyze are not so much due to a misunderstanding of the principles as to their application of them.*

They know, for example, the principle that worship and sacrifice and other acts of devotion directed toward given spirits (whether God or evil spirits) please those spirits. Such worship and sacrifice may enable the spirits to exercise more of their power among humans (always, of course, in the case of evil spirits, circumscribed by what God allows). Such acts of devotion may also quiet (appease) an angry spirit, deterring it from vengeance. In addition to knowing this principle, most of the animists of the world know that there is a supreme God who lives above the evil spirits and is more powerful than they are. They usually reason, however, that the supreme God will be good to them and so they need pay little or no attention to Him. On the other hand, they reason that the way to keep the evil spirits from bothering them is by sacrificing to them to appease them, rather than (as in Christianity) by obeying the God who is above them, allowing Him to protect them from the evil spirits. Though their position is based on a correct understanding of an important principle, and though that position is logical, it embodies a serious misunderstanding of how God intended humans to respond to the very real interference of evil spirits in human life.

We are accused of granting animists enough intelligence to figure this and other principles of spirit world-human world interactions. I plead guilty to this charge. We in the West who have been blinded by a worldview that virtually eliminates the spirit world from our perception have a lot to learn from animists in this area. To be accused of magical thinking, especially of the kind they describe on page 13, however, is hard to take. Perhaps our critics haven't read what we've written, though they claim that a "careful reading" of our materials will result in *their* understandings (even though we can point to many experienced missionaries and others whose understandings of our writings are much closer to ours). Nowhere in my writing or practice, nor in that of the others they critique do we find us accepting or using the magical principles they describe as "the principle of contiguity/contagion and the principle of similarity/imitation." *Nowhere do we contend that either words or material objects have power in and of themselves or that results are automatic if the right formulae are used (as would be true if we were into magic).* In fact, we specifically deny such things (see Kraft 1989:161).

None of us come close to suggesting, as these authors imply "that the efficacy for Naaman's healing resided in the waters of the Jordan, or that the fall of Jericho lay in how many times the Israelites marched around Jericho" (p 57). As throughout their paper, they have "inhaled" their own rhetoric, feeling apparently that their assertion is correct just because they said so, whether or not there is any evidence. I suggest that this is a bigger problem than our guilt for occasionally overstating an anecdote. *We are not embracing animism. We know the difference between power **conveyed** by cultural forms often, as they point out, for purposes of communicational impact and power that is thought to be **contained** in cultural forms.* Even when the latter is the understanding (e.g. by animists), I believe it is an ontological error. That's why I speak of personal beings, demons or angels, as the operatives when objects are empowered.

Words, anointing oil and other items that might be used only *convey* (as did the words of Jesus, the Ark of the Covenant, spit and mud in Jesus' hands and Paul's handkerchiefs and aprons, among other items in Scripture, many of which they list on p 56) the power with which the spirit being (whether God or Satan) that stood behind them invests them. They do not, contrary to the perception of animists themselves, *contain* that power. Our critics need to learn the difference between the empowerment of words and objects that God and, unfortunately, Satan give their followers the authority to convey and the magical concept that things may possess power in and of themselves. There is none of the latter assumption in our practice or writings. By looking only at the superficial, surface-level similarity between the way animists use artifacts and words in magical practice and the fact that we, like Jesus, use cultural forms to convey God's power, our brothers have missed a crucial distinction. *Unless they take note of that distinction, then, they will be found to be accusing Jesus*

Himself of magic and animism for speaking words and using material elements to convey God's power!

Priest, Campbell and Mullen rightly say, "In magic and animism the assumption is that contiguity and symbolic association are themselves the key to power, its transmission, and its effects" (p 57). The problem is, they lead their readers to believe that that is the way we use objects. Right in their statement about animism, way off in their implication concerning us. Then they say, "there is no indication that God required such means for His power to be operative" and imply that we do.   Again their statement about God is correct, the implication concerning us totally out of the ballpark.   In spite of these statements concerning animism on the one hand and God's non-requirement on the other, they go on to make a statement that corresponds well with what *we* believe and teach as if it contradicted us, "In the Bible such associations are there, not because they are necessary for power to operate, but because they are an appropriate and helpful accommodation to communication and interaction with human beings."

But they make no comment on the fact that in the list of examples they themselves cite, power was also "communicated." Indeed, in one of these examples: Jesus comments on the fact that "power went out of me" (Lk 8:46). As with Paul's handkerchiefs (Ac 19:11-12), Aaron's (Ex 7:19-20) and Moses' (Ex 14:16, 21) rods and several other physical objects in Scripture, then, the power flowed through the object used, usually in the person's presence, sometimes in his absence (e.g. Paul's handkerchiefs). They say, "what is key is the faith" of the person healed. Partly right. But there is no automatic, magical power in faith either. The real key is the Source of the power--God Himself--who, in keeping with one of His principles, has agreed to respond to faith in His creatures by communicating/conveying power, often directly, often indirectly through objects and/or words and/or touch--none of them required, none of them powerful in and of themselves (as in magic) but all of them effective conveyances if used under the authority of the spirit being who stands behind them.

Curiously, our critics admit on p 63 that "a demon <u>can</u> enter an object" (emphasis theirs). They then accuse me of implying "that artifacts transmit demons" in spite of the quote they take from me where I say, "artifacts dedicated to enemy gods (spirits) *have demons* in them" (1992:112). Did I say "transmit?" Or did they, on the basis presumably of their "careful reading" of my intent, pull this word out of thin air? They have no case.

CAN ANIMISTS KNOW ANYTHING ACCURATELY?

We are accused on pp 31ff of being so naive that we "assume that the beliefs about spirit realities held by practitioners of occult and animist/folk religions correspond to reality." Then our critics read our minds, claiming that this is our belief "implicitly," give a few illustrations from some of our writings without, as usual showing any of our results, and conclude that the basis for any claim that animists' beliefs correspond with reality is "rooted in the assumption that just as God reveals Himself truthfully, so Satan and his cohorts reveal themselves truthfully" (p 34). Again, their accusations are so wide of the mark that it is hard to take them seriously. For none of us assumes that animistic views of reality correspond exactly with God's Reality (what I call, "capital R Reality"). Nor does any one of us assume that the principles we think we are discovering are the result of satanic revelation, unless that is forced by God, in which case the revelation comes from God even though demons (or humans) might be the vehicle God uses.

In another statement, Priest and his colleagues contend that the Bible "consistently denies that human religious ideas about deities and spirit powers correspond to reality" (p 34). But they admit that it is also scriptural to believe "that when people sacrifice to idols, they are in fact sacrificing to demons" and that in 1 Corithians 8-10 [and throughout Scripture] "the two principles are held in tension" (p 35). If these authors had not presupposed that by granting ontological reality to gods and spirits as demons, we are agreeing with animists in some dangerous way and thereby "incorporating animistic and magical notions of spirit power into our doctrinal understandings" (p 35), they might have seen that we agree with them. They might then have been prepared to recognize that, to the extent that Westerners have dealt with these issues at all, they have focused on the first truth, that these entities are really no threat to God at the power level, only at the meaning level as their followers attribute the meaning "god" to them.

The second truth, however, has been badly neglected by Westerners and needs to be studied. This truth is that genuine satanic power operates in the world through demonic beings who assume the identities granted them by humans (1 Cor 10:20). *By studying and experimenting in this area, far from giving ourselves to animistic beliefs, we are trying to increase the ability of the Christian community to understand a neglected portion of biblical truth.* We are neither turning away from the Bible nor are we naive as our critics contend. We are not granting ontological reality to "folk beliefs about spirits" but to the "actual spirit realities" that all Scripture agrees "are active in the systems of worship opposed to God" (p 35). And we believe animists, though deluded, have as much intelligence as other peoples.

These authors believe that God's principles for the spirit world do not apply in such a way that animists could discover any of them. In fact, they imply, animists are so ignorant that we cannot trust anything they say or believe. Apparently, contrary to our experience in every other sector of life (e.g. science), we can only get truth in this area from interpretations of Scripture and the spirit world developed by (western) Christians. Though Priest, Campbell and Mullen are right that beliefs reflect cultural perception, they assume that those of animists cannot possibly correspond with reality in any way. Animists apparently are so blinded by sin and darkness that we cannot even look to them for clues concerning spirit-world realities. The culturally conditioned perceptions of the authors, however, are assumed to correspond with God's Reality because (they assume) those perceptions correspond with what is taught in the Bible. In addition, they assume that biblical peoples who assumed territoriality of evil spirits are wrong and, therefore, not to be taken seriously simply because the Scriptures teach that God is over all (p 35).

I, and those on my side of these issues, assume that God is indeed over all but that there is a sphere of influence allowed by God to Satan and his spirit kingdom. Like everything else in the universe, then, Satan's kingdom works according to principles that God has laid down. And many of these principles can be discovered by us or by others. Those of us who have interacted with nonwestern peoples with respect to disease and medicine have discovered that animistic peoples have been able to learn some important things about these areas of life. I assume, therefore, that they have also been able to discover some important things about the spirit world and its operations. Not that we can accept their (or our) understandings of the spirit world uncritically. But to simply dismiss those understandings, as Priest and colleagues have, as totally within that area of cultural perception that does not correspond in any way with God's Reality, is going too far. There are intelligent people in animistic societies who have for generations been working with and studying spiritual power. And, like nonChristian (even demonized) scientists in western societies, they are able to discover important truths, even though they then use them in wrong ways to serve the wrong king.

So, I/we believe in going beyond the overt statements of Scripture, though not outside the bounds of Scripture, whether in dealing with the material and human worlds or in dealing with the spirit world. I/we also believe in experimenting with the insights of others, such as animists, those in Scripture who did not obey God, and even (though carefully) demons, in our quest to discover more of what the Holy Spirit wants to teach us in this area.

HERMENEUTICS

Whatever our agreements, and they are many, how we interpret what we deal with will continue to hamper us unless we come to agreed-on understandings of each other's positions. Hermeneutics, however, is a subcategory of worldview. And, though we who write here are in the process of a major worldview shift, we have not as yet been able to sort out all of the pertinent issues. The issues I tackle in the next few sections are hermeneutical issues.

It is clear to most of us that our traditional western worldview patterns affect our understandings of reality in such a way that the existence of invisible things is denied unless "proven" by secular science (e.g. germs, radio and TV waves). Though this is changing a bit as westerners become more interested in and often involved with the occult, our unfamiliarity with the spiritual realm makes us very insecure in our quest to accept and understand more of spiritual Reality. Though we have now gotten over the habit of denying spiritual Reality, since this is such unfamiliar territory, we risk the temptation to overemphasize it (e.g. a demon under every bush) or to accept insight from the wrong sources (e.g. animists). So we fear this tendency in ourselves and others and distrust others if they range farther into this realm than we do. Priest, Campbell and Mullen show this kind of fear and distrust toward us who are named in their chapter.

An important problem in our attempts to make sense out of these matters stems from the nature of Scripture. Throughout Scripture we are given bare-bones, surface-level descriptions of events, usually without any attempt to explain what the motivations were of the persons involved or what were the underlying spiritual dynamics. We are left to infer both. Whether it is Peter's denials of Jesus (Mt 26:69-75) or David's sin with Bathsheba (2 Sam 11) or the reason for Daniel's praying (Dan 10) or why, contrary to Jewish custom, Jesus needed to go through Samaria in John 4:4 or the motivations behind hundreds of other events, we are usually not told what the biblical characters were thinking or even what God was thinking.

Likewise, with regard to the spiritual dynamics lying behind such human events. Except for the conversation between God and Satan concerning Job (Job 1) and that between Jesus and Satan at Jesus' temptations (Lk 4:1-13), we are left to speculate concerning what Satan is doing in the background. We have very little direct information concerning how he operates or the rules by which his activities are governed. Jesus tells us that people are in captivity to him (Lk 4:18-19), that he is the ruler of the world (Jn 14:30), that Satan has a kingdom which, Jesus infers, is active and well-organized (Mt 12:25-26). Jesus demonstrates that His, and the power He gives us (Lk 9:1), is greater than that of Satan's kingdom and calls even a physical healing a release from the enemy's grip (Lk 13:10-17). But neither Jesus nor the biblical authors who record the events explain the principles behind them.

Due to the surface, human-level nature of the descriptions, we often can at least infer the influence of human sin in the events. We are shown, for example, that Adam, David and many others disobeyed God and sinned, thus bringing about judgment by God. But when the disciples attempted to infer sin as the cause of the plight of the man born blind (Jn 9) or of those killed when a tower fell (Lk 13:4), Jesus denied that that was the reason, but gave no insight into the behind-the-scenes spiritual dynamics that influenced these events. Nor are we informed as to why curses and blessings work, when they work and what might be the conditions under which they might not work. Proverbs 26:2 helps a little but does not explain most of what we would like to know. Nor do the descriptions help us much in our attempts to understand the principles in cases such as Jacob's blessings (Gen 48-49) or of the curse God led Elijah to put on Ahab's family because of what he did to Naboth (1 Ki 21:20-24) or of the strange dynamics involved in Balaam's activities in Numbers 22-24 or in scores of similar scriptural events.

One thing that is clear, however, is that our western worldview greatly interferes with our attempts to gain insight into the spiritual realities lying behind such events. From the perspective of our western evangelicalism, we can read the descriptions and easily pick up the human factors. Given our worldview blindness in the spiritual area, however, our instincts are untrustworthy when we try to understand what is going on in that area.

Another important (and rarely noticed) western worldview influence is our habit of reducing every effect to a single cause (see below). In dealing with demonization, for example, a question I am frequently asked is, Is this a demon or a psychological problem? The underlying assumption is that it is one or the other. People frequently are pushed into cognitive dissonance when I reply that it is both. For demons must have something to cling to. They are like rats which cannot exist unless there is garbage to feed on. The "garbage," then, is usually emotional or spiritual damage. So with respect to demonization there is dual causation. Likewise with regard to the issue of "territorial spirits." The argument against praying against (or, rather, taking authority over) higher level demons is often couched in either/or terms. For example, many will say (as have Priest and his colleagues) that we ought to deal with sin and repentance *rather than* with higher level demons because these are what cause the real problems. We contend, however, that there is a dual causation to these higher level problems just as there is in the individual demonized person. That is, dealing with territorial spirits automatically means that we need to deal with the "ground level garbage" of sin that requires repentance. We are not, as our critics would see if they read our materials carefully, guilty of their charge that we are turning people away from the scriptural mandate to deal with the internal stuff. We are simply saying that spirit problems, whether individual or group (i.e. "territorial") need to be dealt with at both human and suprahuman levels.

Among the crucial hermeneutical issues we need to deal with are 1) The place of experience in the interpretation of Scripture and life, 2) How we handle experiential data that has no analog in Scripture, 3) How we apply our interpretation of Scripture to our interpretation of experience, 4) How we interpret the relationships between what happened long ago as presented in Scripture and what happens today, 5) How we handle the blinding effects of western worldviews on our understanding of the spirit world and 6) Whether or not God has left for us to discover at least some understandings of the spirit world through extra-biblical experience, just as He has done with understandings of the material and human worlds.

There are, in addition, certain hermeneutical issues in the anthropological area. Chief among them is the question as to whether the criticized practices are rightly seen as animism and magic. If so, how does one keep from leveling the same charge at biblical peoples including Jesus? How we see the cultural issues, then, interacts with our understandings of how God has set things up in the universe and how Satan, whom we know is an imitator, is able to work. If, as I contend (1994), the rules of operation in the spirit realm are largely the same for both sides (as they are in the material and human realms), it should not surprise us if the forms by means of which spiritual power is conveyed are the same for both God and Satan. For example, the Law of Gravity and all other physical laws apply to both the righteous and the unrighteous. *The major differences, then, in the operation of spiritual principles lie in the source of the power and the way they are used, not in the principles themselves.* In application of these principles, then, the methods and techniques used by Satan and those used by God for blessing, healing, dedication, worship and the like will be largely the same, in spite of the fact that the empowerment comes from opposite sources. Though we use such terms as "animism" and "magic," to designate the satanic use of certain spiritual principles, we should not assume that those principles, put into creation by God Himself, cannot be used (with some differences to be sure) under the power of God for the purposes for which He originally intended them.

THE PLACE OF EXPERIENCE IN INTERPRETATION

The authors of the critique take a standard evangelical position with regard to the untrustworthiness of experience (perhaps because experience from this perspective tends to be falsely equated with feeling). But that stance is based on the myth that it is possible to interpret Scripture in some objective way without reference to one's own life situation and experience.   This, of course, is impossible unless one simply accepts someone else's interpretations based on that person's experience. All interpretation, whether of Scripture or of life, is closely tied to experience, or lack of experience. We believe the experiences recorded in Scriptures are endorsed by God as conveying His truth and, therefore, to be regarded as authoritative, though not exhaustive. But as soon as we interact with the Scriptures, the understandings that we derive are subjective and pervasively affected by the perspectives we bring to the process of interpretation--perspectives strongly influenced by experience.

As I have said elsewhere, there are at least three kinds of knowledge: intellectual, observational and experiential (1989:94). Though as westerners, we tend to understand knowledge as an intellectual thing, the consistent emphasis of both OT and NT is on knowledge based on and validated through experience (see Kittel on *ginosko*). How are we to know, then? It is experience that is the measure, whether we are focusing on knowing God in a redemptive relationship, knowing the truth (Jn 8:32) or knowing what is involved in the four areas of our practice most questioned by our Columbia brothers: the empowerment of objects, curses, the possibility of inheritance of demons and territorial spirits.

A major flaw in the Priest et al presentation is that they cite the things we say as if there were never any results. They completely ignore and avoid any theorizing as to why there are positive results when we experiment with our theories. And they advance no alternate theories to explain our results. Are we so wrong that we are deluded in the hundreds of cases of demonization that we have dealt with? If so, how do they explain what we think we did that resulted in these people getting free from something?   Are we completely deluded when we act on our principles and there are NT-like results? If so, what is their explanation of the results?

Another thing they miss is that ours is not a hopeless message concerning objects, cursing, inherited demons and territorial spirits. This would be something to be really concerned about. Our message is, rather, a hopeful message concerning the authority we have in Christ to reverse disastrous experiences or to avoid them in the first place. They give the impression that we are bent on upsetting the Christian community by propounding theories that will do just that. On the contrary, we are trying to solve problems that are reported from every side.

They contend that they are not rationalistic yet convey western rationalistic bias every time they try to deal with spiritual power. They have, apparently, had little or no experience with what the Holy Spirit is doing even in our society and, therefore, no basis for interpreting His activities either in Scripture or in other cultural contexts. They refer to words of knowledge as "geiger counters"! Spiritual discernment seems outside of their experience.

HAVE THEY REALLY OVERCOME RATIONALISM?

Our critics claim on p 39 that they are biblical, not rationalists. Given the way they treat this subject, however, that claim has a hollow ring to it, given their propensity to consistently deny supernaturalistic explanations either of our experiences or of biblical passages. And the fact that they cannot distinguish between animism and Christian authority makes us suspicious that their claim to have gotten beyond enlightenment thinking is bogus as well. They allow supernaturalism in theory but, apparently, not in practice. That sounds like a variety of enlightenment rationalism to me.

One place where they tip their hand in this regard is where (pp 42-46), in order to avoid granting validity to our results, they state, "On occasion, God works supernaturally even when the method is clearly wrong." This is, of course, true, as they illustrate in the case of Moses and his striking the rock. To infer, however, that God is simply humoring us merely underlines the weakness of their case. We are to especially pity poor Ed Silvoso (p 42) who doesn't know that his (and many others') supernaturalistic methods have nothing to do with the incredible results in Argentina. It's too bad we cannot count on fruit to validate method. Perhaps we should stop, or ask the permission of these skeptics before we attempt to engage in spiritual warfare so they can advise us against it like Priest advised the Aguaruna man (p 42f). Priest allows, though, that it might have worked to allow Anquash to continue to believe that demons were involved.

But he caricatures the advice we might have given, suggesting that our approach would have been to instill fear rather than, as we would have done, to instill the confidence that, should there really be an *iwanch,* now or in the future, going to God for protection is the answer. And it wouldn't mean scheduling an exorcism or moving out of his house, it could be done on the spot. With Priest's rationalistic approach, however, it is very likely that either Anquash or someone else in his group later did something spirit-related in secret from the gringo that satisfied their traditional conceptions of the spirit world but also gave evil spirits more power over them. Priest missed a golden opportunity to work *within* their categories (whether or not these corresponded with Reality) to assist that group to employ the power of God (whether or not there actually was an *iwanch*) in a very biblical way. The teaching from 1 Corinthians 8 and 10 could also have been given but, since Paul's teaching seems to be contradictory (compare 1 Cor 8:7 with 10:20-21), it could be balanced with the more typical teaching on the subject of food offered to idols from Revelation 2:14, 20, Exodus 34:15, Ezekiel 22:9 and, of course, 1 Corinthians 10:20-21. And Priest should have taught what we would have taught (though, as usual, he misrepresents us as holding the opposite), that "merely physical contact with either [meat or houses] is not what makes one vulnerable to demons" (p 44).

While teaching on these subjects, he might have mentioned that even rationalistic, American Christians believe enough in the power of God to dedicate their babies and their church buildings. Pastors dedicate their sermons. Some western Christians even pray over their homes in the belief that God honors such dedication of places. And some, conscious of the fact that Satan is constantly active in a world called his by Jesus (Jn 14:30), even regularly claim His protection and obey Paul's injunction to put on God's armor (Eph 6:13) because we are at war with unseen beings whose job is to harass and destroy us if possible. What an opportunity was missed to work within Anquash's meaning system to teach him something biblical about spiritual power so that perhaps he would not, like most of the Christians in the two-thirds world, continue to follow the traditions of his ancestors whenever a spiritual power problem arises! Of course, I don't know that Priest's rationalistic method didn't have good long-term results. I pray that it did. Maybe it worked even "for reasons other than those assumed by [the practitioner]" (p 44). But I do know that his approach has been a major reason for the dual allegiance problem throughout the Christian world, since spiritual power issues are not dealt with or, as here, explained away, leaving Christians to deal with these issues according to animistic tradition, since there is no help within Christianity.

Meanwhile, back at home, our critics are correct when they assert that "many missionaries have rightly come to realize the need for rethinking their poorly thought through understandings of demonic realities" (p 10). This rethinking, then, as they point out, leads at least some of us to experience a paradigm shift and, I would add, the even more influential change I call a "practice shift" (see Kraft 1989), leading to "a radical reorientation of their understandings of spirit realities and a radical rethinking of ministry strategy in the light of these perceived realities" (p 10). The fact that such paradigm shifting has led to widespread sharing of the insights coming from new (to us) experiences is what concerns these critics. Instead of lauding the fact that we are writing about our experiences and opening up the subject for public discussion, Priest, Campbell and Mullen act as if we are doing something wrong. They seem disturbed that we are not conducting "business as usual," but, rather, like those seeking better ways of doing things, are attempting to share, compare and stimulate more creative thinking within the evangelical community. As late twentieth century missiologists, we have a pretty good idea of the kinds of approaches that don't work. We believe that such new approaches as we are advocating deserve to be tested. There will be mistakes, there always are. But continuing to ignore the existence and effectiveness of the satanic kingdom is one mistake we have chosen to stop making.

As for the paradigm shift itself, these critics say, "If the paradigm shift being advocated involved an unadulterated return to biblical supernaturalism, we would applaud it. But we fear that such is not the case" (p 11). I'm afraid, though, that the tone of their chapter indicates that they probably would not even recognize such a shift if one occurred. They seem a long way from biblical supernaturalism themselves when they misread us as advocating animism and miss completely the differences between animism and our use of delegated authority, when they fail to rejoice with us over the fact that many of those we have ministered to are now free and when they call for a return to "productive reality-based understandings and methods" (p 24). Judging from this presentation of their stance, the understandings and methods they recommend would be naturalistic rather than spiritual.

The contention that "some missiologists are promoting a pre-scientific and magical worldview rather than a biblical one" (pp 12) is an interesting one, especially since biblical worldviews are themselves pre-scientific. We are thus accused of advocating one pre-scientific worldview by those who claim to be advocating another, and with the assumption that a scientific worldview (presumably secular and naturalistic?) would be better. The accusation doesn't make sense and, in any event, is wide of the mark since the discussion is over different understandings of what is biblical, not whether or not we are pre-scientific. Our critics have grasped at the wrong straw in raising this issue.

On another issue, we are accused of "privileging" the understandings of "the weaker brothers" and, indeed, of "helping to plant such 'weaker brother' meanings in a mind that did not formerly think in those terms" (p 45). This is a difficult accusation to deal with for at least two reasons. First, the accusation flows from the assumption that only one of the two apparently contradictory things Paul says in 1 Corinthians 8 and 10 about food offered to idols is correct. But second, there is a sense in which we *are* attempting to help the weaker ones who are in difficulty because they are afraid rather than confident in their relationships with the spirit world.

Paul's point is that strong Christians do not need to fear the influence of an enemy kingdom that is infinitely less powerful than the Kingdom we represent. We do not, therefore, need to go around fearing the very real presence and influences of the enemy kingdom. Though we should recognize the demonic presence enough that 1) we do not partner with the enemy by eating and drinking at his table (1 Cor 10:20-21) and 2) do not, because of our security and confidence, mislead weaker Christians into putting the wrong meanings on our activities and, by imitating us, to fall into sin (1 Cor 8:9), we should not let ourselves become fearful and disabled by our awareness of the activities of evil spirits.

I don't believe it is better for us to allow weaker Christians to remain ignorant of spirit-world realities (as our critics seem to favor). Nor is it wrong to risk a bit of misunderstanding in order to help the weaker ones to discover their spiritual authority and to move into the kind of security Paul is advocating. We are to be secure enough both to claim God's power for protection, whether unconsciously or consciously (i.e. through prayer, 1 Cor 10:30), and to behave in such a way as to accommodate to the weakness of the less secure. In this way we handle effectively both the meaning and the empowerment issues. We who are attacked have chosen to try to help people break through both ignorance and fear of spiritual Reality to security in the little understood (by western Christianity) power area.   The meaning area has been studied by evangelicals for some time now.

What we could have wished for is that these authors would first have tried to understand what things might look like on our side of the paradigm shift and then have raised their issues (even the same ones) in a context of mutual trust, rather than of fear and mistrust. Instead, they seem to know what the Scriptures say and imply whereas we don't, they couldn't possibly be misleading their followers whereas we are and their understandings and methods are "reality-based" whereas ours are completely off the track because we are pragmatic and experience-oriented. Results, of course, don't count because the future will prove that they were merely temporary psychological phenomena, based on the credulity of people who attributed meaning to false understandings of reality. Such denigrating of experience and results, of course, is hardly "reality-based." In fact, in most areas of life, results are greatly preferred to mere theorizing.

A SCIENCE IN THE SPIRIT REALM?

Though there are obvious differences between the position I and the others who were challenged espouse and that of Priest and his co-authors, I believe we all share the common goal of sincerely seeking the truth. We also seek to go about such a quest in a structured, organized, rational manner--as scientists do. When there is such a wide difference in experience, however, there will inevitably be major differences in interpretation of certain scriptures, of certain phenomena and of at least certain aspects of life itself. This makes for the liveliness of scientific discussion.

This is a process that involves give and take, the advocating and testing of positions and the questioning of them by those with a different point of view and experience. And we agree with these critics that "such testing is a biblical demand, not evidence of enlightenment unbelief" (p 39). Their unbelief becomes evident, not in the call for testing but in the fact that they seek to discredit those tests, unscientific and anecdotal though they may be, that seem to confront their enlightenment assumptions.

Those of us from evangelical, non-charismatic backgrounds have generally not dealt with the kind of issues before us. Personally, I tended to ignore them, as did my seminary professor who allowed the Systematic Theology course to end before we got to the section in the textbook that dealt with Satan and demons. Those from Pentecostal and charismatic backgrounds often functioned in this area but without a major concern for comparing notes in a systematic way and analyzing the broader issues involved. It is, however, a new day in this regard. For one thing, some of us non-charismatic evangelicals with at least as strong a biblical orientation as the Pentecostals and charismatics but with behavioral science training and orientation have entered the arena. And some of us have garnered considerable hands-on experience in addition to the bent for analysis we bring to the subject. In addition, there are an increasing number from Pentecostal and charismatic backgrounds interested in analyzing and comparing notes.

These factors, plus the increasing openness of both sides to each other's perspectives, put us in a better position than ever before to develop the kind of dialogue that could produce a science in the spirit area parallel to the physical and human sciences we already have. If we recognize, as I think we must, that there is a third area of Reality (the spirit realm) parallel to the Reality of the material and human realms, then there must be in that realm a large number of regularities that can be studied to produce insight into the rules ("laws") by means of which the spirit realm operates. The process by means of which we discover these rules and the results of that process will someday (hopefully) constitute a much more complete science of the spirit realm than we can point to now. We are probably at this point, however, several hundred years behind those who study the material world in our attempts to understand this area of Reality.

If we are to develop such a science, there are certain crucial areas of discussion that need to be sorted out. The first and most important of these is the issue of trust. We need to trust each other even to the extent of trusting the validity of each other's experiences and analyses. It is clear from the chapter by Priest and colleagues that they do not now trust those on my side of the fence. Whether or not we ever come to agreement, we need to listen to each other in an attitude of trust and openness to learn. An adversarial position, motivated by distrust and fear, will cripple our discussion from the start.

There are a considerable number of issues on which we probably agree. Among them are the authority and trustworthiness of Scripture, the existence of the spirit world and its constant interaction with human beings, the inadequacy of our western worldview to enable us to fully understand what's going on in the spirit realm, the need to seek understanding in this area and the need for those concerned to compare notes and to thereby enrich each other.

Among the hermeneutical issues mentioned above is the problem of how much we are to be limited to Scripture in our quest for understanding of the universe in which we live. Prior to Galileo's time, it was common for Christians to assume that all that God wants us to know about the universe is embodied in the Bible. Those who, like Galileo, claimed otherwise were harshly treated by the Christian establishment. Nevertheless, they persevered in the conviction that humans could learn much about how the physical universe operates through scientific study of that world itself, quite apart from and beyond the small amount of information provided for us in Scripture. And they proved their point.

Now we laugh at the naiveté that restricted those who sought to explore, theorize, test, compare and continually replace older understandings with newer ones.   Though we don't accept every theory that scientists advance concerning the universe, we honor the process by means of which we have gained an incredible amount of insight into and control over the universe.

Likewise, with respect to the quest for understanding of human beings.   Though again, we don't accept every theory coming from psychologists, sociologists, anthropologists, political scientists, historians, communication specialists, linguists and the like, we recognize the great value of their insights even when they go far beyond what the Bible has to say about humans.   Could it be that there are principles and regularities in the spirit world, just as there are in the material and human worlds, that God has left for us to discover outside of Scripture?   If so, could this be why one of the Holy Spirit's assignments is to lead us into further truth (Jn 16:13)?

I believe that all parts of the universe--the material part, the human part and the spiritual part--are governed by God according to rules and principles that He has embedded in His creation.   Some, but not all, of these principles are indicated in the Bible.   The rest are left for us to discover.   And just as during the years since Galileo people have learned that it is profitable to explore the material and human dimensions of the universe, so we are learning to explore the regularities in the spiritual world.

Priest and his colleagues are working on the assumption that truth in the spiritual area, unlike that in the physical and human areas, must all be derived from Scripture.   This is the attitude the Medieval Church took in opposition to Galileo and the other round earth advocates.   Those who opposed Galileo assumed that God had revealed all there was to know about the physical universe and that any search for understanding based on experiment and experience was, therefore, invalid.   Our assumption is that God has not revealed all there is to know in the spiritual area any more than He has in these other areas.   We, therefore, need to experiment in this area and, like scientists who work in other areas, develop and test theories in order to gain greater understanding.

In a discussion such as this there are two attitudes we can take toward the use of Scripture.   We can contend, as Priest, Campbell and Mullen have, that ideas and/or practices are scriptural only when they are explicitly condoned and/or taught by Scripture (according to one's own interpretation).   Or we can contend that ideas and/or practices may be scriptural as long as they are not condemned by Scripture.   Though these authors take the first position, we take the second and feel we have the right to experiment and develop theories on the basis of those experiments in an attempt to go at things scientifically. We welcome, then, interaction even if it knocks down some of our theories. I believe all of us would welcome attempts beyond our own to measure "the effects of spiritual warfare types of counseling," evangelism and any other dimension of our approach (p 41), as long as it is done sympathetically rather than simply to knock down something that doesn't happen to fit a critic's paradigm. It is unfortunate that these critics do not so much interact with our theories as to deny them. Perhaps in another go around, they could experiment with our approaches to test them out for themselves. If this would happen, we would be on a totally different basis for our discussion.

USE OF ANECDOTAL EVIDENCE

Are we anecdotal? Of course. But so is Scripture. And so are our critics, at least the few times they point to any data at all. At least we have presented some data. That's what makes it possible for those who disagree with us to critique us. It's a shame they haven't taken us or our anecdotal data seriously enough to interact with it apart from their misplaced accusations concerning us and animism.

Do we base interpretations of Scripture and of contemporary events to a large extent on our experience--or, rather, on our understandings of the interaction between the stories (anecdotes) of the experiences recorded in Scripture and our own? Yes, of course. But so do Priest, Campbell and Mullen.   As I've already pointed out, the interpretations of our critics as well as ours, whether of Scripture or of life, are thoroughly affected by experience, even in the face of their claim that theirs (but not ours) are "biblical."   When we've experienced a large number of the kinds of things we tell the stories (anecdotes) of, though, we begin to see patterns emerge. This is the data we work from. It would be nice to have controlled experiments to point to. But we are not at that point yet. I am, however, more optimistic than they are concerning the possibility of conducting such experiments in ways similar to the ways in which we do behavioral science research (p 42). These would at least point to probabilities, if not allowing us to come to precise conclusions. Meanwhile, we describe occurrences in ways similar to the way Scripture describes them, leaving people to infer what is going on.

Those of us who have been criticized have a mountain of data to point to. It is not clear what, if any, data the Columbia scholars are working from. If they have data, it would be helpful if they would suggest alternate theories and approaches based on that data. The few stories they record in their chapter are seldom even helpful in supporting their points. In addition, they need to deal with our data. They cannot simply sweep it under the rug (as they have done) because they don't happen to believe that God would fill teeth (p 36) or lengthen legs (footnote 23) or empower objects (p 14ff) or work more on one side of a geographical border than the other (p 40). Pragmatism may have its flaws but when all you have to combat it is theory based on prejudice, pragmatism based on experience wins hands down. It may "not seem overly impressive" (footnote 23) for a leg to be lengthened, unless it happens to be your leg and you no longer have a back problem because God did something, even if it was to back muscle rather than to leg bone. And if God did seem to work more on the Brazil side than on the Argentina side of the border, that data cannot be dismissed as lightly as Priest and colleagues have simply because it is old, the one who reported it "could not recall the name of the town" (footnote 16) and some of those who have referred to the event have misinterpreted or misreported parts of the story.

Can they explain the phenomena we are describing and the results in a better way? If so, let them do it so we can all learn from their valuable perspective and insights. Given that our critics provided no data in any of the areas they criticized and advanced no alternative analyses of our data, I suspect that they are critiquing us from a base of little or no experience and, therefore, of little or no knowledge. Simply taking potshots at us from behind some facade of experience-poor, theoretical understandings of Scripture is not helpful (not to say unfriendly). Remember that John 8:32 refers to experiential knowledge, not mere theoretical knowledge, as that which undergirds the truth that sets us free: "you'll *experience* the truth and the truth will set you free" would better capture the emphasis than the conventional renderings.

With full understanding that experience can be misinterpreted, we look to quantity of experience and consistency of results to bring a measure of protection. When, then, we find that a technique works consistently, this experience enables us to develop a theory based on an interpretation that provides guidelines for the next time we encounter a similar situation.

Having said that, I would like to apologize for some of the stories we have used and to comment on a few of those they selected. Though all of us are anecdotal, if we are to get beyond the name calling stage, we do need to learn how to use our stories and illustrations better. We should not simply look for the opposition's wildest story and/or claim and, as our critics have done, castigate the whole movement on the basis of one or two stories. Personally, I regret Wagner's use of the Sumrall illustration (pp 46-48) and resent the implication that all of our data is of this nature. I'm sure Wagner will be more careful in the future, since there is no dearth of illustrations in this area. As for McAll (1991) and the Bermuda Triangle, I know of none on our side of the fence who agree with his belief that the spirits McAll claims to have sent away were those of the people who were killed there. My view is that if the problems McAll cites were caused by spirits, these would have been demons carried by the murdered slaves which, instead of going somewhere else when their hosts died, stayed in the vicinity of the bodies they once inhabited.

With respect to the remarks by Dawson and Otis concerning times when they felt the presence of evil, we need to take seriously the caution concerning the untrustworthiness of feelings. Similar feelings and, indeed, similar intensity can come from several sources, including culture stress, other emotional states and God Himself. We do, however, need to recognize that some people are more sensitive to possible perceptions of evil spirits than others. And it is likely that the gift of discernment is broader than the rationalistic interpretation our critics give in footnote 21. Probably God is not as concerned as Priest and his colleagues to maintain the neat division they try to make between mind and emotions. If God has gifted certain people with any kind of discernment, and I believe He has, He (not the demons, p 52) might just send a signal to them through their emotions. He might even gift certain people with discernment that they experience primarily in the mind and others with heightened emotional and/or spiritual perception.

With regard to some of Murphy's statements, I have already suggested that I hope I can be more careful in the future than he and I have been in the past. I can understand how an assertion that "there is no reason to doubt [the demons'] claim" (p 31) can upset our critics, especially if Murphy did not go on to show a correlation between what he thinks he found out and how God used that information to set a captive free. On the other hand, since our critics refuse to believe our theory that demons can be inherited, no matter how much evidence pointing in that direction we can supply, it may not be so important for them how we state our case. For those who are more open minded, however, we need to be more careful.

In any event, all of us need to be more careful in our use of anecdotes. But, if Wagner and the rest of us are wrong to suggest that, like the Flat Earth Society, some "already have their minds made up" (p 38), what shall we say about these authors who, with mistrust and negative presuppositions firmly in place, have tackled us? I apologize for any negative statements or innuendoes I may have been guilty of. I would, however, suggest that these authors apply to themselves their plea that "pejorative labels" and "polemic" be avoided in favor of "a direct and honest interchange of ideas and arguments within the context of peer review " (p 39-40, footnote 15)." I see none of the latter in their piece. Maybe next time?

TALKING TO DEMONS

Priest, Campbell and Mullen critique me/us for "interviewing" demons. Their *theory* is that since demons are liars, they can never ever tell the truth and, therefore, never be of help to us even under pressure from the Holy Spirit. From the certainty with which they present their theory, one might suspect that they have tried getting information from demons and found that they have always been misled. I doubt very much that that is the case, however. I suspect that they are working from theory alone (a very unscientific way of going about things), without the benefit of experience. But we have in Scripture a record of Satan himself telling the truth in tempting Jesus (Lk 4:1-13). Though he was trying to deceive Jesus, he was telling the truth when he pointed out that Jesus had the power to turn stones into bread and that God would send angels to protect Him if He jumped from the temple (Mt 4:1-7). Jesus, of course, under the guidance of the Holy Spirit was wise enough to call Satan's bluff. It was in the experience of a conversation with the evil one that an important victory was won. The Holy Spirit still is able to give such guidance, enabling us to defeat the enemy by using against him the very information he gives us.

Though the way I obtain information from demons is not strictly parallel to what went on in Jesus' conversation with Satan, the latter shows at least two things that we have found true--demons *can* tell the truth and we, under the authority and power of the Holy Spirit, can, like Jesus, control the situation. What I have found consistently is that the Holy Spirit forces them to reveal to me information concerning what we need to deal with to weaken and get rid of them.

Since, when there is demonization, the real problem is not the demons but the emotional and spiritual "garbage" in the person's life that gives the "rats" a legal right to live there, the information we seek concerns those root problems. I don't simply converse with demons for the fun of it or to obtain general information--though a good bit of such information, whether accurate or inaccurate, comes along the way. The whole purpose for talking to demons is to use them to obtain the information we need to get people healed and, in the process, to get rid of them. And if they reveal something that, when we use it, enables us to defeat them (often with people with whom others, using other methods, have failed), we are grateful for the way God uses this technique.

Our critics don't like me talking to demons. It doesn't fit their theory. But they don't mention that my experience (as recorded in my books) is 1) that the Holy Spirit is the One in charge when I get information from demons, 2) that I am careful to never let them take control and 3) that lots of the things the demons say under pressure from the Holy Spirit prove out. And people get free. Our critics must deal not only with the practice they don't approve of but with the results of using that practice.

The data I advance to back my claim that this is an effective method consists of between 400 and 500 positive deliverance sessions-- sessions in which demonized people were freed. And we could at least quadruple that number if we counted the experiences of my associates. To counter my practice, these authors need to explain the fact that over and over again the Holy Spirit seems to lead us to crucial insights through the statements that He forces demons themselves to make.

Might it not be parallel to what happens in court when a "hostile witness" is put on the stand. By definition, a hostile witness is trying to support the other side. Thus, the aim of the attorney who is questioning hostile witnesses is to entrap them into revealing information that will help the attorney's (not the witness') cause. Nobody has suggested that our judicial system not make use of hostile witnesses simply because we can't trust them. Everybody knows, though, that they and their statements need to be handled carefully. An important factor creating a difference between using a human hostile witness and using a demon is that the power of the Holy Spirit adds to the pressure in remarkable ways.

Do we naively trust everything these hostile witnesses say? Of course not. I've said that. But do we believe the power of the Holy Spirit is great enough to get liars and deceivers to help us? Yes. And we've seen it happen over and over again. Risky? Yes. But there are an awful lot of people now free of demonic interference in their lives because we risked it, trusting not the demons but the Holy Spirit. If our critics can come up with a technique that works better for those of us who don't get all the information we need through words of knowledge, I wish they would share it with us.

It is a curious thing that our critics are so confident that God has the power to do anything He wants to in most areas but, apparently, He can't force demons to help us. We are told that God can let us know all we need to know about demons (p 30). He *can* indeed. But *experience* tells us that He often does not do things according to our rules and expectations. Our critics believe, then, that Satan and his helpers are too much for God.

Apparently, even God doesn't have the ability to make demons tell the truth, ever! Priest, Campbell and Mullen are concerned about truth, so are we. When, then, we get information from demons under the influence of the Holy Spirit, that checks out as the truth, the source of the revelation is not, as they contend, demonic. The demons are only the means. The source of the truth is God.

As I have stated in a chapter on this subject in my book, *Defeating Dark Angels*, I do not enjoy talking to demons. Nor do I trust them without checking up on them. And I am not as confident as Murphy that I can always keep them from lying. It is important, though, to control things (in the power of the Holy Spirit) and not allow them to do what they want to do. When we "interview" them, we put them completely under the authority of the Holy Spirit. A typical question I ask is, "Does this person need to forgive anyone?" When the answer is "Yes," I command them to tell me who it is the person needs to forgive. The demon usually tells us the name. And usually it is someone the person has forgotten about. When, then, the person forgives the one named, it becomes obvious that the demon's power is lessened and we are able to free the person both from the demon and from the sin of unforgiveness that gave the demon his rights.

If we can get this kind of information in any other way, we do. Often God reveals such information either to the person or to me through a word of knowledge. If not, though, getting it from the Holy Spirit through His pressure on the demon is a good second choice. And it has so far enabled several hundred people to be freed from demons who probably would not have been freed is we refused to use this disagreeable method. I am reminded of the story of someone who criticized Moody for some of the methods he used in evangelism. If I remember correctly, his reply was something like, "I don't always like my methods either, but I like the way I'm doing it better than the way you're not doing it."

I have found, further, that others who, like me, don't have spectacular spiritual gifts, have been able to learn how to use enemy spirits in this way to obtain the information they need to bring freedom and healing to many Other models of deliverance, though they may work reasonably well for the more gifted among us, don't seem to be as teachable as this method. But note that our aim in getting such information is not simply deliverance. As I explain in my books, my aim is to get the person free from the spiritual and emotional "garbage" that gives the demons rights and then, usually as a second step, to cast out the demons.

Is this the way Jesus did it? No. At least as far as we can tell from the Scriptures. Though, as I've already pointed out, Jesus did converse with Satan himself. I have on occasion been able to cast out demons His way--by simply commanding them to leave. But more often,

He seems to lead me and my colleagues to obtain and use information provided by the demons themselves. And if this method means there will be a freedom smile on the victim's face afterwards, I'll gladly use it, whether or not the inexperienced theorists like it.

DUAL CAUSATION

A major problem in the Priest, Campbell and Mullen chapter is that the authors are committed to either-or thinking. They suggest that we are off the track in looking for spirit-level explanations when, they contend, Scripture puts the blame on human sinfulness. While it is true that Scripture emphasizes the fact that we are sinful, even to the extent of describing our hearts as deceitful and "too sick to be healed" (Jer 17:9). In addition, nowhere does Scripture release us from responsibility for our sinful choices. This part of the NT perspective is what Kallas calls "the Godward view" (1966).

But there is another perspective that Kallas claims is even more prominent in Scripture. He labels this perspective "the Satanward view" (1966). The presence in Scripture of these two perspectives side by side, the one requiring full responsibility on our part for what we do about our sinfulness while the other represents humans as to a large extent victims of an enemy who is too big for us, is perhaps the greatest paradox of Scripture and the Christian life. Both perspectives are present in Jesus' words and works. Though He held people (especially those who, like the Pharisees, had studied the Scriptures) responsible for their own choices, He never condemned anyone for being demonized or ill. He simply rescued them as if they were helpless victims. As evangelicals, we have learned well the "Godward" perspective. We have, however, largely remained ignorant of and puzzled over the part Satan plays in the universe.

Scripture tells us, however, that there is an enemy who is very active and whose commitment is to "steal, kill, and destroy" as much as possible in the human context (Jn 10:10). And we are expected, like the NT Christians to "know what [Satan's] plans are" (2 Cor 2:11). When Jesus announces His reason for coming to earth, He speaks of humans as "captives" and "oppressed" (Lk 4:18-19). He later refers to Satan as "the ruler of this world" (Jn 14:30). Both Jesus and the NT writers were very conscious of Satan's activities in the world--much more conscious than we seem to be. Paul calls the enemy "the ruler of the spiritual powers in space" (Eph 2:2) and points out that "we are not fighting against human beings but against the wicked spiritual forces in the heavenly world, the rulers, authorities, and cosmic powers of this dark age" (Eph 6:12). Peter, then, describes the enemy as one who "roams round like a roaring lion, looking for someone to devour" (1 Pet 5:8).

When dealing with the demonic, though, we soon learn that we have to work at both the human and the spirit levels. Priest and his colleagues, in keeping with standard evangelical doctrine, emphasize the fact that our problems are rooted in "Satan's influence in the doctrinal, moral and spiritual arena ... sin and deception" (p 23), not in the enemy's ability to empower curses. What they don't seem to see in our writings (perhaps we haven't stated it as clearly as we should have) is the fact that we are attempting to understand the dual causality of Scripture. Everything that happens needs to be seen at both levels--though there are human causes for most things, there are also influences coming from the spirit level.

As I have indicated above, demons can live in a person only if there is something within that person for them to attach to. This can be sin, though, as I have indicated (in a passage they referred to without dealing with the context, 1992:47ff), most of the Christians I work with have already taken care of things ordinarily thought of as sin. It is more often something like unforgiveness, wallowing in anger, deep feelings of rejection, lust or a number of other conditions that may rightly be called sin but usually are not thought of when that term is used. Or, we theorize on the basis of a mountain of data, there may be an inherited satanic grip stemming from ancestral vows, curses, dedications or sins (see below for defense of this theory). Whatever the garbage that gives the demons their rights, we need to speak of two causes (garbage and demons), not just one.

Likewise, with respect to cosmic-level relationships between human and spirit beings. In order for higher-level spirits (I prefer this term to "territorial spirits" for reasons given below) to have influence, there needs to be some vulnerability at the human level. When, therefore, there are groups of people usually organized in territorial groupings (e.g. nations, cities), institutions, businesses, clubs and the like promoting racism, occult involvement, pornography, abortion, homosexuality, gambling or any of a number of other sinful activities, they are giving higher-level spirits legal rights in their society. Just as there are two causes to deal with in demonization, then, with higher-level spirits we need to deal with both the human and the spirit world concomitants if a problem situation is to be rectified. For example, it is critical that people repent of, say, racism, if the power of the higher-level spirits whose job it is to keep the sin active is to be broken. So we can speak here also of dual causation.

I contend, therefore, that no spiritual problem is completely analyzed until both the human level and the spirit level causes are taken into account. Throughout the Bible, especially the OT, whenever a battle (whether group or individual) takes place, it takes place on both levels. An individual is tempted: there are both internal factors stemming from his/her sin nature and external factors stemming from the fact that the members of the satanic kingdom, "the spiritual powers in space" (Eph 2:2), are always there to empower temptations. The Israelite army takes on the Philistines at the human level. The God of the Israelites takes on the gods of the Philistines at the spirit level.

A startling example of this need to recognize and analyze causality at both human and spirit levels is recorded in 2 Kings 3:24ff. Israel is defeating the Moabites to such an extent that the latter are driven back into their walled, capital city. The Moabite king, in desperation, took seven hundred of his swordsmen and tried to force his way through Israel's lines (v 26). But in vain. "So he took his eldest son, who was to succeed him as king, and offered him on the city wall as a sacrifice to the god of Moab," and Israel was routed (v 27)! Why? At the human level, Israel was winning in a big way. The king of Moab, however, through the sacrifice of the heir to the throne, was able to throw so much spiritual power at Israel that they turned and ran, without, sadly, remembering that they could have appealed to a greater spiritual Power and won at the spirit level as they had been winning at the human level.

Such an example witnesses, I believe, to a rule of the universe: that humans can cooperate with spirit beings, enabling them to do more than they would otherwise be able to do. On the Christian side of the fence, we can, through prayer and obedience enable God to do His will. Those who obey Satan, then, enable him to get his way (within the limits set by God). There is, I believe, continuous interaction and quite a bit of interdependence between humans and spirit beings on both God's and Satan's sides. When we obey God, He is able to do more of what He wants to do. And when we fail Him, His will may not get done (unless He overrules). Thus, Jesus prayed that God's will would be done "on earth as it is in heaven" (Mt 6:10) because it is not automatic. He does not want any to perish (2 Pet 3:9). But, apparently, His will will be partially thwarted in this matter due to human lack of obedience. Dual causality.

In spite of what we've said concerning the need for something at the human level to enable spirit-level activity, there is also some degree of activity possible, independent of human permission. We would contend, for example, that God can, probably still within the rules He has put into the universe, exert influence on people who seem, at least, to have no use for Him (e.g. the conversion of the Apostle Paul, Nebuchadnezzar). God can restrain, protect and attack within those rules. It should not seem strange to us, then, that Satan, working under the same rules though not with the same degree of autonomy, can exert similar kinds of influence in the human arena. We have the example of Job, where God was protecting him and Satan requested and received permission from God to attack him, even to the extent of killing his family (Job 1:1-2:10). Interestingly, though, the enemy allowed Job's wife to live in order that she could be the vehicle to convey Satan's message to Job--"curse God and die" (Job 2:9). This part of the story shows dual causality: Satan gave the words (see his prediction in Job 1:11), Job's wife spoke them.

Satan also tried to kill Jesus as a child (Mt 2:16). In order to do this he linked up with a human, Herod, who would do his will by ordering the killing. God, however, was able to communicate with Joseph and Mary through a dream, instructing them to flee to Egypt. In both cases there are spirit and human components to the events. Dual causality.

I contend, then, that the rules of the universe allow Satan a certain amount of autonomy to exert influence both on those who serve him and, to some extent, on those he does not have rights over. With Job, he requested and gained more rights than were his previously. With us as sinners, he has certain rights because of our sinful condition. As a part of his right to tempt us, he seems to be able to put thoughts into our minds. Apparently, he also has the right to test us and perhaps even, on occasion, to capture us, judging from the words Jesus used in the Lord's Prayer: "Do not bring us to hard testing, but keep us safe (deliver us, NIV) from the Evil One" (Mt 6:13). Satan's ability to influence both "pagans" and the people of God, then, is abundantly clear from the OT, as well as from contemporary experience.

In any event, our attempts to understand and analyze need to take account both of the human and the spirit influences on any given situation.

THE FOUR FOCAL ISSUES

1. INFESTED OBJECTS

Our critics don't like the idea that objects can carry spiritual power. As usual, they provide a caricature of what we say. We never say that God requires objects "for His power to be operative" (p 57), or that mere "physical contact with [meat and houses] ... makes one vulnerable to demons" (p 44), or that a Christian's security depends on "residing in safe places where demons cannot reach us" (p 44), or "that demons need objects to gain power in people" (p 45).

Again, though, we have a lot of before and after data that suggest that the action taken provides the reason that a given kind of demonic harassment stops after certain objects are either disposed of or prayed over. We tentatively conclude, then, that the objects were infested. Indeed, Wagner himself experienced this problem first hand. After his wife, Doris, had experienced demonic presences several times in their own home, they invited two people with spiritual discernment, of the kind Priest, Campbell and Mullen deny, to enter their house to discern what needed to be done. Though, because of the spiritual power emanating from the house (presumably because the spirits knew why these two had come) they were at first unable to enter the house, they finally got in and were able to identify some objects the Wagners had brought home from Bolivia as at least partially responsible for the problem. These objects were destroyed and the Wagners have had no such problems for the last ten or more years (Wagner 1988:63ff).

Probably all of us who deal with demonized persons have had the experience I have had on several occasions of getting nowhere with a demon until the person removes some object. Often this is a necklace, a ring, sometimes a Masonic ring, or some other item of jewelry or decoration. As soon as the item is removed, then, experience has proven that our ability to deal with the demon is immediately improved. Usually when we ask the person about the item we find that it has been blessed (with satanic power) and given to them by someone in an occult organization.

As Priest knows, the form-meaning distinction is an important one in anthropology. We often use the term "form" to label a cultural item. The item may be a material object (e.g. jewelry, a house, a chair, an idol) or a non-material entity (e.g. a word, a ritual, baptism, a song). All of the visible and invisible items of culture are forms. People observe and use these cultural forms. People also interpret and assign *meanings* to these forms. And, as our authors point out (pp 44-45), the meanings people assign to cultural things can affect them powerfully. In their desire to explain our contentions about the empowerment of cultural forms naturalistically, then, Priest and his colleagues attempt to attribute everything to the meanings people assign to them. Though, as I have stated, meaning can be a powerful thing, our experience leads us to recognize a third component (in addition to form and meaning) that has to be taken into account with cultural forms that have been dedicated to spirit beings, whether God or Satan.

When an object is dedicated to God or to Satan (usually in the name of a god or spirit), a meaning is given to it. But it cannot be meaning alone that explains the ability of such an object to hinder the casting out of a demon, for seldom does the person wearing the object have any idea that it can affect the process. So we postulate that the assumption held by those who dedicate such objects to their gods is accurate--that the objects receive some kind of ability to convey the power of the spirit to whom it is dedicated. We call this ability "empowerment." In many societies, implements used for food getting, warfare, religious practices and other necessary activities are routinely dedicated to clan spirits when they are made. Traditional peoples living on South Pacific islands, for example, dedicated their canoes when they made them. Temples, homes, workplaces and whole nations (e.g. Japan) are also dedicated by priests with the authority of their gods behind them. We believe they are thereby empowered, enabled as conveyances for spiritual power.

An anecdote--I once foolishly visited a temple in Taiwan during an important festival honoring the spirits of death and came away with a severe pain in my chest that was not relieved until three weeks later through prayer. Perhaps it was chance. Perhaps the event is explainable on the basis of meaning alone. Perhaps. It is curious, though, that with me and with many others who have recounted similar experiences to me, the problem started at a specific time related to a place that just might have been empowered and ended at a specific time related to the application of the greater power of God to the problem. In this case and the many others I have heard (including the items in the Wagners' home), it takes less faith to believe in this type of empowerment, which we believe is biblical, than to postulate that meaning or simply chance are sufficient to provide explanation. Naturalism requires great credulity.

Even western Christians dedicate church buildings, the elements of Communion, anointing oil and babies to our God. In addition, we bless individuals and, in benedictions, whole congregations in the name of Jesus Christ. Though our critics probably believe such dedications and blessings are merely empty rituals or significant only because of their meanings, I don't. I believe these acts have meaning, of course. But multiple experiences when blessing or anointing a person has produced an immediate and unexpected reaction have convinced me, in spite of a good bit of skepticism, that we are also dealing here with God's empowerment. The effect of blessing and dedication on buildings and babies is more difficult to demonstrate but enough anecdotes can be collected in this area to point strongly in that direction (at least for those open to such a possibility). For we have the authority of Jesus Christ Himself to speak God's power through blessing and dedication. This is not animism, though a superficial reading of it might lead to that interpretation.

Our critics observe correctly that empowered objects are frequently mentioned in Scripture and point out that those references indicate quite a different understanding of the relationship of power to the objects than is true of an animistic interpretation (p 57). They are right.

They are, however, so enmeshed in their misanalysis of our practice, teaching and writing that they assume we are on the animism side of the equation when, in fact, we are on the scriptural side. Whether the power comes from God or Satan, the empowerment comes from outside of the object, flowing through it. It does not come from the object itself even when animists analyze it that way. Priest, Campbell and Muller rightly say that "in magic and animism it is the external forms--the objects and symbols themselves--which are key" (p 58).

Nowhere, however, will they find us believing what animists believe in this regard. They have not found a single quote in our writings to support their point. In fact, we agree with almost everything they say on this point except the statements and inferences that we are guilty of animistic thinking. There is even less evidence that we are reading the Scriptures "through the lens of a magical/animistic worldview" (p 61) than that they are reading them through a naturalistic, rationalistic one. Our authors' footnote 24 is an interesting one, added probably in response to a criticism of their original paper. They disclaim using the term animism only for affect, then repeat their definition (they had no definition in the original). Since it is clear they are using the term for affect, they would have a better case if they had left out the definition. By their definition we are simply not guilty and definitely not "teaching people to think about demonic power in terms of [the contiguity/contagion and similarity/imitation] assumptions" (p 61, footnote 24).

On p 45, it is inferred that we are teaching "that demons *need* objects to gain power in people" (emphasis mine). We, of course, teach no such thing and disagree strongly with the statement. What we say is that, like Jesus, enemy spirits can *use* objects to convey their power. And, even when animists misinterpret the source of the power as the object itself rather than a spirit that uses the object, it is the spirit being that empowers.

This statement is made in the context of a discussion of the importance of meaning in dealing with occult objects. Our critics say, "When an object has occult meanings for an individual, any failure to repudiate and get rid of the object is indicative of divided spiritual allegiance ... [and] gives Satan an opening and must be renounced. The danger lies, not in physical contact with a physical object, but in how a given individual treats an object which has occult meanings for him" (p 45). I agree with most of this statement but hold that satanic power is wielded through more than meanings. It is not mere meanings that we wrestle with (Eph 6:12).

2. WHAT ABOUT CURSES AND BLESSINGS?

As for cursing, Priest and his colleagues accuse us of advocating something we do not advocate, based on the animistic principles we do not hold. They call the way we use words in the authority of Jesus "verbal magic." They contend that we believe in "a kind of natural efficacy to curses" in which "the power resides in the formula or in the technique" (p 65). They accuse me of claiming that the power to curse "is now our own" (p 65). But if they read what I say without their overriding presuppositions, they will discover that my whole emphasis with respect to both cursing and blessing is on our right to use the authority God gives us to operate in His power. The danger I point out is that we may employ the power of God under the authority God gives us to hurt through words that curse rather than to help through words that bless.

As we do when we send a secretary or other employee to carry out a task, God gives His followers a sphere of authority. He expects us, then, to use that authority within the guidelines He has set for us, not all of which we know. Within that sphere of authority, then, we have a certain amount of freedom. But that freedom, apparently, can be misused without God withdrawing it. It appears that a fair number of God's servants have used the authority He has given them to serve ends other than His. So, indeed, it is with Satan who was given a certain amount of authority and power as one of God's highest angels but then chose to use them to oppose God, the Source. It looks to me as though Satan has been able to keep the power he used to have as an archangel, even though he is using it against God. There is probably a principle here, related to God's patience and respect for free will.

The point we make is exactly what they assert when they say, "God, or God through His spokespeople, may choose to exercise His power in certain contexts by verbal curses, by touch, or by mixing saliva with mud and applying it to blind eyes. But the Bible never teaches that the power resides in the formula or in the technique ... The power is God's" (p 65). We only teach what they state but are accused of teaching that there is some power in formulas or techniques! The thing they assert that they don't seem to factor in is that God uses "spokespeople" (us), people to whom He has delegated authority to assert power "in Jesus' name and by using Jesus' methods, including blessing and, I'm afraid, cursing.

If we have no such ability, why does Paul command us to bless rather than to curse (Rom 12:14) and James warns us against the fact that blessing and cursing can come from the same tongue (Jas 3:9)? As throughout their piece, our critics take no account of the authority relationship we have with God. Jesus has delegated to us authority over demons and diseases (Lk 9:1), authority to bless (Lk 10:5-6) with its inverse the authority to curse and authority to forgive (Jn 20:23).

The same kind of authority we have with God, then, is given by Satan to his followers, since the rules are the same. They, therefore, also have the ability to "bless," curse, heal and do miraculous works (Mt 24:24) in the power of their master. Perhaps the clearest scriptural indication of the power Satan's followers can wield is given in the record of Moses challenging Pharaoh in the early chapters of Exodus. For the data, see Exodus 7:12 (sticks into snakes), 7:22 (the Nile to blood) and 8:7 (frogs).

Though, as our critics have rightly pointed out, we cannot trust feelings, I have had many occasions when I have used the authority of Jesus and blessed people and they have immediately felt whatever it was that I blessed them with. When one has worked extensively in the power of God, it is easier to believe that at least many of these are the result of God's power rather than purely psychological.

Priest, Campbell and Mullen are troubled by the suggestion that even Christians can be affected by curses. Since curses are the inverse of blessings, and people can be affected by blessings, I feel I must believe in this possibility. The only question is, Under what conditions? We take Proverbs 26:2 to indicate that for a curse to affect a person, it must "connect" with some vulnerability inside him/her (e.g. sin or other spiritual problem such as demonization). And those we have ministered to who suspected they had been cursed, with a few puzzling exceptions, met this condition. I don't know what to do about the exceptions except to suggest either that they are really not exceptions (i.e. there is something we don't know that puts them in the above category) or for some reason God gave permission (as with Job) for a curse to get through. The ideal would seem to be what Jesus was able to say of Himself in John 14:30: The ruler of this world is coming *but he finds nothing within me to connect with.* However, it may have been a curse that God let through that occasioned Paul's "thorn in the flesh," a problem that Paul refers to as "a messenger from Satan" (2 Cor 12:7). There would have been many who directed curses at Paul during the course of his ministry.

Again, blessing and cursing are scriptural concepts, not merely animistic ones. And what we practice and teach bears no resemblance to our critics' definition of animism and magic.

3. TRANSMISSION OF DEMONS GENERATIONALLY

This is a condition I do not like at all. But I have been involved in casting out too many demons of Freemasonry and other occult and nonChristian religious involvements from people *who themselves have had nothing to do with that organization* to avoid it. These are people whose father, grandfather, mother or grandmother (or sometimes a lineal relative even farther back), not themselves, have been members of the organization. To instance Freemasonry, since that's the one I have had most experience with, as members, Freemasons take vows that dedicate themselves and their descendants (often unconsciously) to Lucifer as a part of the rituals they go through (see Decker 1992; Shaw and McKenney 1988). I have to ask, Did these folks pick up the demons through family contact alone? This theory would work for some. But for many, their contact with a grandparent who was a Mason was minimal. The most likely theory, as distasteful as it may be, seems to be inheritance.

A second bit of evidence is found in the fact that when we take authority over the person's ancestry, using the power of Christ to break generational curses, vows, dedications and the rights given the enemy through sin by the person's ancestors, the demon's power is often virtually gone. This frequent experience suggests either that the demon was inherited and has power through the family connection or that some tendency was inherited that gave the demons rights in the person.

As in most of what I've said above, we are simply calling them as we see them in our experience. I invite anyone reading this, especially our critics, to enter into such experiences and see how they call them. Perhaps there are better theories out there. I, for one, would welcome them, especially in this area. It is, however, not going to work to simply deny as our critics hint at doing (p 26, footnote 10) that we are actually dealing with demons. The kinds of interactions we have with them, including the interviews, are very convincing, even to those skeptics with open minds who have watched and listened as we have worked to get captives free.

As for the contention on pp 22-23 that we are advocating "the idea that our vulnerability to the power of demons is based on nonmoral and nonspiritual conditions," again our critics have failed to see some crucial points. First, as throughout Scripture, we are finding we have to deal with sin, spiritual and moral issues as humanity-based, not just individual-based. This means that, though such problems as demonization are indeed the result of sin, the sin that gave the enemy his rights may have been that of someone in authority over an individual (often a lineal relative or an abuser) rather than that of the individual him/herself. As with sin in the case of the man born blind (Jn 9), the demonized person may not be personally to blame. And, in fact, as Priest, Campbell and Mullen have noted (pp 22-23), many of the demonized who have come to me, are not in their condition because of individual moral or spiritual rebellion. They have already, through confession, taken care of their individual sin problems but, through no fault of their own, still carry demons that entered from some other cause.

A second point, though, is that, even when the original source of the demonization is inheritance, there is usually emotional and/or spiritual garbage to deal with. Though this garbage may have come after the original infestation through inheritance, it appears to be this factor that can give opportunity for demonization to come about through curses (Prov 26:2) or *external* influence of demons to occur through contact with infested objects. I am not saying, as Priest and his colleagues imply, that demonization occurs through "inadvertent contact with some object" (p 22).

Thirdly, I am saying, as they assert, that Satan has the "ability to attack based on factors other than our doctrinal, spiritual or moral response" (p 23). We certainly see this ability demonstrated in Job's life, with Jesus and with Paul's thorn in the flesh. We live in a world where he is called the ruler (Jn 14:30; 1 Jn 5:19; 2 Cor 4:4). This understanding and the laws of the universe that give Satan the right to attack us, his enemies, however, cannot simply be dismissed as "magical and animistic thinking." And the conditions under which such attacks can occur cannot be oversimplified to be "based on conditions of physical contiguity and symbolic association with words, objects, persons, and places" (p 23). In the face of spirit-world realities, whatever they are, we need to work in both of the ways our authors suggest: in trust, we should "seek to live lives worthy of the God who called us" *and also* "devote attention and energy to the effort of decoding" whatever the conditions might be that allow satanic interference in our lives, even if the need for the latter introduces "a measure of spiritual insecurity" into our lives. *It is out of a need to seek answers to the kinds of spiritual problems that remain even for those who are very successful in living godly lives that the kind of attention we are giving to the latter issues has developed.* And we are experiencing a measure of success which *may possibly* mean that we are not as totally wrong as Priest, Campbell and Mullen contend.

In any event, we are not advocating, as they infer, that missionary strategy be turned away from any of the good things we are already learning and doing. We are, however, recommending that we add to the useful human strategies that I, Priest and others have been teaching a serious attempt to factor in spiritual warfare issues. We have learned that culture is not the enemy. Now we must learn how to fight the real enemy who works within the cultural context. This is an attempt to increase the coverage of "reality-based" strategies, not to turn away from them.

4. TERRITORIAL SPIRITS?

Given the spiritual realities we've been discussing, it doesn't seem to me too far fetched to speak of a satanic "force field" influence over people who live in territories. Note that when we refer to territories, we are referring to *the people* more than to the geography. As throughout the OT, starting with Adam's sin, continuing through the murder of Abel and on throughout Israel's history, the sinful acts of humans brought curses on the geography in which those sins were committed (see Gen 3:17; 4:10 and frequent references thereafter to spiritual damage to the land). So we (and probably Priest and colleagues as well) believe the geography is affected by the behavior of the people, both past and present. In keeping with the spiritual warfare theme of Scripture, then, we hold that the nature of the effects of such sinful behavior is to give a personal being (Satan) rights over the land. Contrary to our critics' misinterpretation, we see no automatic, animistic, "electrical," impersonal power here, except as it flows from the person of Satan. We believe, rather, that just as the Fall gave the enemy certain rights, so contemporary or past human sin, especially the sin of allegiance to Satan, gives him rights.

In spite of the impression our critics give, by the way, I don't use the term "force field" except in this context--to refer to satanic, not automatic or magical--power wielded over a territory . Whether "territorial spirits" is the best name for this factor or not is an open question. My preference is for another term, since this one puts territory in focus rather than the people who inhabit that territory. As with Adam and Eve, though, human disobedience to God may give the satanic kingdom certain rights to territory. The Fall gave the enemy general rights as he points out to Jesus in Luke 4:6 saying, The kingdoms of the world and all their power and wealth "ha[ve] all been handed over to me, and I can give [them] to anyone I choose." This is a territorial outcome even though it was people who handed over the territory. And it is continuous, affecting generation after generation until Jesus comes to take it back.

Recognizing the fact of Satan's authority over the world plus the fact of the organization of his kingdom into something like the Eph 6:12 hierarchy (it may be a hierarchy in spite of some of the commentators) leads many of those who ponder the situation to postulate satanic rulers over territories, especially over the people who inhabit the territories. This theory gains support from the observation that there are particular groups of people committed to particular types of evil and that there seem to be concentrations of sinful institutions and/or organizations in particular localities. For example, though it might be chance, I think we can assume that Satan is smart enough to be behind the fact that businesses promoting such things as drugs, pornography, prostitution, gambling, occult bookshops and the like often congregate in the same locales. And, as John Dawson (1989) and others (Wagner ed, 1991) point out, a look at the history of many of these places draws attention to the fact that these very locales have usually been specifically committed, often formally dedicated, to satanic influence in earlier generations. Is it unreasonable to suggest, then, that such a regularity tells us something about how the spirit world interacts with the human world?

And then there are the experiments (e.g. Argentina) in which both Satan's power over a territory or group of people and the ground-level human sins are dealt with and a great response to the gospel results. Though our critics have done an impressive amount of reading on these subjects, they don't seem to have taken into proper account the results of this approach in Argentina and, lately, in several other places through Ed Silvoso's seminars. In this area as well as in the others under discussion, the results we see from our approaches seem to be less relevant to Priest, Campbell and Mullen than their presuppositions.

Spiritual mapping, then, is a contemporary form of spying out the land (Num 13). Just as Moses was instructed by God to send spies into the Promised Land to discover whatever could be discovered that would help them later when they attempted to take it, so the advocates of spiritual mapping suggest that we "spy out" whatever we can to discover the ways in which the enemy is working in any given area. Though some may make unwarranted claims for this approach, common sense suggests that we investigate and experiment with seeking to discover whatever we can that will aid us in promoting the cause of our King. We believe God would rather have us experiment with new approaches than to retain our present level of ignorance. Whatever the outcome of the investigations and whatever the claims made for this approach, I believe we can learn from Scripture that the prayer that is integral to the approach is a right thing to do.

PRACTICAL IMPORT OF IGNORANCE

Our critics are concerned (rightly) about the implications of our approaches for the Christian community in general and for missiology in particular. Unfortunately, since they pay virtually no attention to our results, these authors give the impression we are going around scaring people needlessly. If dolls given as gifts to missionaries can carry demonic power, they state, missionaries who dispose of them might be "hindered in their ability to enter fully into reciprocal relations with those to whom they go" (p 22). Then they go on for a few more pages to elaborate their fears that anyone would take us seriously and experience "spiritual insecurity" (p 23) and devote time and attention to dealing with satanic power that we say can come through curses, objects, inheritance and infected territory. People should, rather, devote their "valuable energies and resources [to] productive reality-based understandings and methods" (p 24). To buttress their point, then, they give a couple of illustrations of people who in ignorance overreacted. Apparently, neither they nor the ones who advised them knew how to employ the authority granted us by an all powerful God who loves to be called on to protect and deliver us from such problems. We think it is important for Christians to learn how to work in that power and authority.

One important advantage to working from experience rather than simply from presupposition is that we can usually get beyond the fear these critics rightly want to avoid to provide answers to many (unfortunately, not yet all) of the problems raised by the recognitions they are afraid of. We do not, as these critics imply, simply scare people by advancing theories without showing what to do about the problems we identify. For example, I can point to several adoptees and their parents to whom I've ministered whose whole lives have been changed when we worked on the assumption that the adoptee had inherited a demon and we employed the power of God (usually in the process talking to the demon) to get rid of it. It is possible that there is another explanation for what happens in cases like these. But until one is discovered, we work with the understanding that works, whether or not our critics like it. Additionally, I have worked with several people who regularly experienced demonic presences before they disposed of objects we suspected were infested but who have had no such experiences since disposing of them. Is there another explanation for the change in their situation? Or have we come upon an aspect of truth we didn't know before?

These authors are afraid that people who read our materials will become fearful of demonic activity in and around them. This, of course, is a very real possibility. And it would be tragic if what we are dealing with is not true, as they assert. Our experience, however, is that far from becoming unbalanced by our approach to ministry, most of the people we minister to are finding answers to problems they've already been experiencing. And they are getting freed from them by the power of a Christ who is like the Jesus of the NT, rather than like the powerless one they've known before.

It is, however, an unfortunate fact of modern life that books published and lectures given are often only partially digested. For this reason, some go off on tangents--just as some did in response to Jesus,

Paul, the Bible and any other new information that was spread widely. As Christians, we believe we should let the world know the message of salvation, a message that involves the bad news of sin, death and hell. And many misinterpret what we proclaim. Is this, then, sufficient reason to disobey Jesus by refusing to proclaim the Christian message? Of course not. Neither does the fact that some misinterpret, even become fearful, because they have not properly understood deter us from working with Jesus to set the captives free (Lk 4:18-19)

As I have written elsewhere (1992:104ff) it looks as though the enemy's first line of defense is ignorance. If, then, he can't keep us ignorant, he tries to get us to fear. Our critics seem to feel that we should not teach and write about the subjects they don't like because it might be upsetting to the Christian community. They, however, don't face, as I do on almost a daily basis, people who are struggling in evangelical ignorance to overcome attacks of the enemy coming from each of the areas they have critiqued. If they did, they might have to, as I do, pray hard and try some experiments that seem "off the wall," even sometimes disagreeable (e.g. that Christians can be demonized and that we can obtain valuable information from demons) and find that they work. In actual experience, we have seen a lot of things change when we work on the basis of the theories our critics attack. For it is a fact that in the *real world* it is how theories prove out in practice, not simply how reasonable alternate theories sound, that carries the day. And we have a mountain of data and experience to support our claims. This is a surer way to the kind of "productive reality-based understandings" (p 24) they are calling for than their method of picking apart someone else's methods simply because they don't trust us.

Nevertheless, let the discussion continue. We will continue to be practitioners. We will continue to fight ignorance and seek truth, then, both from experience and from our critics always, with them, holding ourselves accountable to God. As we do this, then, we will endeavor to teach and write enough to help our hearers/readers through both the ignorance and the fear barriers to the victories that come in the application of the love and power of God to situations of satanic captivity. I am sorry about the persons they cite who approached their problems with ignorance and fear. They could have been helped by reading some of our writings.

CONCLUSION

Priest, Campbell and Mullen have set a dangerous precedent. Things could have been a whole lot different if they had first tried to understand us and to enter into dialogic interaction over the issues that concern them. Or if they had been working from more than a bare minimum (if that) of experience. It certainly could have given a more honest picture if they had dealt with our results, many of which we supply, as well as with their concerns and tried to explain these positive results on the basis of some other theory than ours. As it is, the presentation raises within those of us on my side *the specter that there might be people who read their materials and hear their lectures but not ours who might be misled into thinking they are portraying us accurately.* Some might even take their accusation that we are into animism seriously because they too do not understand the differences between animism and Christian authority and/or they too are working purely from theory without benefit of experience.

They have challenged me/us and charged us with heresy. I hope I have been able to demonstrate that their charges are poorly grounded, due to 1) a lack of experience in relation to the spirit world and 2) a poorly developed supernaturalistic perspective that together partially explain several additional problems including 3) a lack of understanding of the differences between animism and Christian authority which, in turn, contributes to 4) difficulty in interpreting those of us they critique, 5) certain portions of Scripture and 6) those experiences of life that involve supernatural beings and power.

REFERENCES CITED

Cabezas, Rita
>   1992   *Struggling Against Demonic Principalities.*   Published
>   privately (Aptdo Postal 21, Plaza Gonzalez Viquez, San
>   Jose, Costa Rica, 1001).

Dawson, John
>   1989   *Taking Our Cities for* God.   Lake Mary, FL: Creation
>   House.

Decker, Ed
>   1992   *What You Need to Know About Masons.*   Eugene, OR:
>   Harvest House.

Good News Bible: Today's English Version
>   1976   American Bible Society.

Kallas, James
>   1966   *The* Satanward *View.* Philadelphia: Westminster.

Kraft, Charles H.
>   1989   Christianity *With Power.* Ann Arbor, MI: Servant.
>   1991   "What Kind of Encounters do we Need in our Christian
>   Witness," in *Evangelical Missions Quarterly* 27:258-65.
>   1992   *Defeating Dark* Angels. Ann Arbor, MI: Servant.
>   1994 (ed) *Behind Enemy* Lines. Ann Arbor, MI: Servant.

Kraft, Charles H. and Marguerite G. Kraft
>   1993   "The Power of God for Christians Who Ride Two
>   Horses," in *The ingdom and the Power.* Gary S. Grieg
>   and Kevin N. Springer eds.Ventura, CA: Regal, pp 345-
>   56.

McAll, Kenneth
>   1991   *Healing the Family Tree.* London: Sheldon Press.

Shaw, James D. and Tom C. McKenney
>   1988   *The Deadly* Deception.   Lafayette, LA: Huntington
>   House.

Wagner, C. Peter
>   1988   *The Third Wave of the Holy Spirit.* Ann Arbor, MI:
>   Servant.
>   1991 (ed) *Engaging the* Enemy. Ventura, CA: Regal.

3

BIBLICAL INTERCESSION: SPIRITUAL POWER TO CHANGE OUR WORLD

Patrick Johnstone[1]

INTRODUCTION

What a privilege to be brought into the Kingdom for such a time as this! Never before has the Church of the Lord Jesus Christ grown so fast or extended its witness so far. The tide of the Gospel now laps at the final bastions of the enemy of souls. World evangelization is a foregone conclusion because of God's promises.[2] The world, as we see it, is a battlefield at every level—political, moral, mental and spiritual—with many strongholds to be stormed. His infernal majesty is not a "push-over" and in recent years the nature and intensity of the spiritual warfare in

---

[1] The author, Patrick Johnstone, served for 16 years with the Dorothea Mission as a missionary evangelist in the poor urban areas of South Africa, Zimbabwe, Botswana and Mozambique. During this time he learned something of the spiritual warfare needed to see people steeped in witchcraft and the occult come into the liberty the Gospel proffers those who truly repent and believe in the Lord Jesus Christ. Also during this time he commenced the task of compiling data and information for the writing of successive versions of Operation World (Johnstone: 1974 - 1993). He is now serving with WEC International as part of the leadership team of the Mission-Director of Research, 1980 -   and Deputy International Director 1986-1992. He is also Chairman of the Unreached Peoples Network of the AD2000 and Beyond Movement.

[2] Numerous Scriptures assure us of the final victory achieved through Jesus in His death and resurrection and applied by us: Matt 24:14; Matt 28:18-20; Psalm 2; Dan 2:44; Dan 7; Rev 1, 5, 20-22, etc.

which we are engaged has become more apparent. Yet, for these seemingly impregnable strongholds to fall, we must wield those weapons given to us by God.

There are two extreme approaches which can impair our effectiveness in the spiritual warfare associated with world evangelization:

1. Under-emphasis of the spiritual nature of the conflict. For too long Western Christianity has done just this and many missionaries have gone into situations ill-prepared for spiritual opposition (Neil 1990:13). This was certainly my experience in Africa. I was working among a people steeped in witchcraft and the fear of spirits. I owe much to my godly African co-workers who educated me about the spiritual powers at work and their cultural setting. They also demonstrated how the Lord Jesus gives total freedom through a deep repentance with renunciation of the works of darkness and faith in Him.

2. Too great a preoccupation with the enemy. There has been a rapid growth of awareness of, and fascination with, the occult. This, together with the infiltration of New Age Hinduism, has radically changed the world-view of many in the Western world. As a result people have become far more conscious of these spiritual forces. We easily become too devil-conscious and lose sight of the reigning Lord Jesus. The more we know of God, His Word and His power, the better we are able to deal with the enemy. Dealing with the occult can become a morbid fascination for Christians. It can be a dangerous side-track to delve into every form of satanic stratagem and technique to overcome them, for we can become ensnared in time-consuming deliverance ministry or live in danger of unconsciously making ourselves open to the dark powers. Jessie Penn-Lewis's book, **War on the Saints**, which came out of the 1904 Welsh Revival, warns of an over-preoccupation with the things of Satan. Frank Peretti's popular novels on spiritual warfare were written to alert Christians to this unseen conflict. These helped to fill the gap in Western theology with a convincing interpretation of the real world. But despite the author's pleas (Peretti 1989, Wakeley 1995:158) not to build a theology based on these vivid portrayals of demonic forces, we find many readers have. Our Christian bookstores carry a plethora of titles on spiritual warfare, some propounding exotic techniques and speculative solu-

tions. Such extremes can become a divisive element in the Body of Christ. Hence this book.

We need balance and a biblical centrality in our understanding and involvement in spiritual warfare. The authors of chapter one wrote in their introduction: "If the paradigm shift being advocated involved an unadulterated return to biblical supernaturalism, we would applaud it" (p 11). I aim to keep within these parameters, for it is on these parameters that we all should be in basic agreement. I, therefore, deliberately look beyond the basic challenge in Priest's article in the first section on an animistic world-view infiltrating missiology. My aim in writing this section is that we go beyond the present controversy and get on with world evangelization by active intercession for the countries, peoples and cities still in the thrall of the prince of this world. My premise is that we are largely agreed on Scriptural objectives in spiritual warfare and, further, that the means for attaining those objectives may be just as well expressed in the terms used in the Bible. The main means by which this will be achieved is intercession.

Our prayers can change and are changing the world. We do not have to understand everything about the forces arrayed against us, but we do need to understand the nature of the power and authority that is ours in Christ. Sometimes our technical knowledge hinders us. I have been impressed by the increasing concern among Christians for the evangelization of Muslims. Yet, often the best missionaries are the ones who have studied little more than the basics of Islamics but have a passion for sharing Christ. In their boldness for Jesus, they plunge in to witnessing to Muslims where an Islamicist would fear to go. By saying this I am not advocating that a knowledge of Islam is wrong, but we must not let that knowledge cripple our faith that the Holy Spirit can bring about the conversion of Muslims through our witness. The same is true as we confront the devil and his kingdom of darkness and forces of evil. We must not be ignorant of his devices (2 Cor 2:11), but nor do we have to know everything about demonism, the occult, the hierarchies of the spirit world, before we dare bind the strong man and spoil his goods (Matt 12:29). Donald Jacobs, a Mennonite missionary in East Africa, testifies powerfully to the godly balance of African Christians associated with the East African Revival and how their longing was to know more of Jesus and even to turn their backs on the detailed information their traditional religionist compatriots sought about demons (Jacobs 1990:306).

We need the simplicity and faith of children in our waging war against the strongholds of Satan. My late wife, Jill, was long burdened to write a book to help children pray for the world (J. Johnstone, 1993). Its title, **You Can Change the World**, came about in a beautiful way and illustrates this principle. When Jill began to write the book in 1990, she described the land of Albania. The land was then a Communist hermit state which proudly claimed to be the first truly atheist country in the world and where all religious expression was illegal. At our mission headquarters in England there was a group of praying children who interceded for each country or people as Jill completed each chapter. These children took on their hearts the need of the children of Albania where the Gospel was banned with no known believers. They prayed for religious freedom to come to that land. A few months later the Communist government fell, and freedom for worship and witness came. Jill had to rewrite the chapter. When these children heard of the answer to their prayers, they were delighted. One of them shouted out, "We have changed Albania!" That was true, but, of course, they were not the only ones praying earnestly for the Gospel to have free entry to that needy land! Just 4 years later we now know there is scarcely a town left in that land which does not have a group of witnessing believers. May God give us their faith and simplicity. May these words encourage the reader to engage, not in controversy, but the enemy in the combat of intercession![3]

INTERCESSION TO CHANGE THE WORLD

1. The Historical Evidence

a. Great Events Precipitated by Prayer

One day from the vantage point of Eternity, I believe one of the major praise points before the Throne of the Lamb will be

---

[3] My involvement in this project came at the pleading of Dr Robertson McQuilkin, the erstwhile President of Columbia International University. He prevailed upon me to add a final chapter to this book to encourage believers by looking beyond the issues raised in this book.

His working in history through prayer. In fact I see Revelation 5:1-8:5 as a demonstration of this. This is about the seven seals that the Lamb alone could open. The whole section is bracketed by references to the prayers of the saints (Rev 5:9; 8:1-5) and interspersed with paeans of praise for redemption and the Lamb's right to open the seals. The first six seals (Rev 6) show the manner and principles of God's judgments on mankind; Rev 7 shows parenthetically the simultaneous gathering of the disciples from the peoples of the world. Both the judgments and the gathering are the outworking of those prayers. The seventh and final seal reveals the secret of the impact of the prayers of the saints on the world.

I give just three major turning points of history to illustrate the impact of prayer:

The Moravian 100-year Chain of Prayer. In 1727 revival broke out in the Herrnhut community. A prayer vigil was begun then which continued day and night without a break for over one hundred years. Out of this movement of the Holy Spirit a passion for missions emerged. The Moravians became the first Protestant body to specifically commit themselves as a body for world evangelization (Tucker 1983:70-71). Is it surprising, that through the Moravians, John Wesley came into his "heart warming experience of Christ"? This was followed by the great 18th century revival that swept Britain and North America and then led to the modern missions movement. The mighty flow of the Gospel over the past 200 years was birthed and nurtured in a century-long prayer meeting.

The Evangelization of China. Hudson Taylor, the founder of the China Inland Mission, left an indelible mark on Christians in the last century as he emphasized the need for prayer and pled for reinforcements to reach the millions in China's unevangelized provinces (Taylor 1918) China and missions became inseparable in the minds of most believers. Yet, by the time Communism gained control of China's mainland in 1949 and ended all foreign mission work, the response had been relatively small with a total Christian community of about 1.5 million Protestants and about 3 million Catholics. It seemed to the human eye that the Gospel had failed again to penetrate China's heart. It appears that the work God wanted to do was too great to have man taking the glory which may have been the reason all missionaries were forced to withdraw. Over a century of prayer for China was not forgotten and the seed sown in tears and blood was watered by fierce persecution.

During the 1980s we began to be aware that something dramatic was happening as reports began to circulate of millions coming to Christ. Before the 1989 Tiananmen Square incident when the pro-democracy protest was crushed, this movement to Christ had been predominantly rural. Subsequently, the urban and intellectual sections of society were impacted. Reasonable estimates in 1992 for the total community of Protestants was reckoned to be 63 million (baptised believers would be half of this), and of Catholics to be 12 million (Johnstone, 1993:163). The world has never before seen a turning to God on such a scale—a harvest against all the odds through definite intercession for China's millions.

The Collapse of Communism. In January 1984 Brother Andrew, the Director of Open Doors, put out a fervent challenge to the Christian world to pray for seven years for the tearing down of the Iron Curtain and for freedom for the Gospel. The Holy Spirit must have given Brother Andrew a prophetic burden and vision, for within those seven years Communism in Europe and the USSR had collapsed as a viable ideology. The USSR itself had ceased to exist. Now we see the Church growing rapidly in many countries once dominated by Communism. Ideologies and anti-Christian systems cannot withstand the concerted, militant, believing prayers of God's people. Why have we so neglected this ultimate weapon? How long could Islam, Buddhism, Hinduism, New Age, Western materialistic apathy or any demonic empire remain in place with further global prayer thrusts of this kind? All of these religious and belief systems are in opposition to God and seek to deny full freedom to know the remedy in the Gospel. It is the weapon of prayer that will expose their internal contradictions and contribute to God's shaping of events in judgment on them. Paul's words are true in today's world just as they were in biblical times:

> for the weapons of our warfare are not worldly but have divine power to destroy strongholds. We destroy arguments and every proud obstacle to the knowledge of God, and take every thought captive to obey Christ (2 Cor 10:4-5).

b. Great Intercessors Who Changed the Course of History.

In the histories of revivals that have deeply affected the lives of nations and areas, I have been struck so often by the evidence that the Holy Spirit raised up special intercessors who prayed for the fire to fall. To mention a few:

- **David Brainerd** who agonized for the indigenous Americans (Indians) and saw life-changing revival come (Tucker 1983:90).

- **George Müller** who demonstrated that God could be trusted to support thousands of orphans by the prayer of faith without appeals to man. He laid the faith basis for finances for much of the most innovative and effective missions advances that followed (Pierson 1899).

- **Rees Howells** who interceded in the heavenlies for divine deliverances in the darkest days of World War II and saw dramatic answers (Grubb 1952), showing how we believers can change the course of human history.

- **William Duma**, a humble Zulu pastor in South Africa who so walked with God that his prayers led to remarkable miracles, even the raising of the dead, and who gained the respect and love of all races in the darkest days of apartheid. At one time he had the only fully multiracial church in the country (Garnett 1979).

We need many others of like caliber to impact our world.

c. The Great Harvest Now Being Won Through Prayer.

In preparing the latest edition of my book, **Operation World**, I have been awed by the number of prayer requests listed in the 1986 edition which are no longer points for prayer, but rather for praise, because answers have come. The growth of evangelical believers around the world is staggering–especially in the parts of the world where the Gospel was still unknown 200

years ago. Part of our research was to make what is probably
the most comprehensive attempt ever made to analyze the
growth (and decline) of the 25,000 identified denominations, and
the Church, as a whole, over the past 30 years (Johnstone
1993:23-26). Just to quote one statistic; in 1960 the 29 million
Evangelicals in the non-western world constituted about 30% of
the world's Evangelicals; by the year 2000 this could have risen
to 400 million and nearly 80% of all Evangelicals. Consider the
massive turnings to God in Africa in the 1960s, Latin America in
the 1970s, East Asia in the 1980s (especially Indonesia, China
and South Korea), and in the former Communist countries of
Europe in the 1990s. Even in the belt of territory between the
Atlantic and Pacific and the Latitudes 10°N and 40°N–often
called the 10-40 Window–we are seeing the beginnings of an unprecedented harvest. This is true among Muslims with more
coming to Christ individually and as communities than ever before in history. There are also significant initiatives launched for
Hindu and Buddhist regions of the world. There is a worshipping and witnessing group of Protestant evangelical believers in
every one of the 237 countries and territories of the world and
also a church planting movement launched and rooted in over
10,000 of the 12,000 ethnolinguistic peoples in the world.

For the first time in history we can meaningfully speak of
seeing a church planting movement within every ethnolinguistic
people and making the Gospel available for every person in our
lifetime. This has become the driving vision of the AD2000 and
Beyond Movement. I can only attribute these advances as a direct answer to strategic prayer by millions around the world.

I have become aware over the past 20 years of a growing
number of prayer initiatives and networks unprecedented in the
history of the world. There is, in fact, a **prayer awakening** under way, the scope of which would astonish us if we knew the
whole story. The availability of information and the globaliza-
tion of the world missionary force have increased the emphasis
on strategic praying for Gospel advances in unevangelized parts
of the world. What are some of the characteristics of this prayer
awakening?

1. **The intensity** of an early morning Korean prayer
meeting in almost any Protestant church in the country or of the
extensively attended Friday all-night prayer meetings in many
congregations in Brazil.

2. **The militancy** of the praying Christians expecting Satan's forces to yield in power encounters, leading to significant movements to Christ in hitherto resistant peoples. I well remember a Dorothea Mission Week of Prayer we held in the then Portuguese-ruled Mozambique in 1965. To that point little Protestant mission work had been permitted in much of the country. We definitely claimed that land for Christ and an opening for the Gospel. Within weeks, missionaries had gained entry into that land.

3. **The variety of expression** in simultaneous prayer at full volume, prayer walking, marches for Jesus, hands raised to heaven, lying prostrate before the Lord.

4. **The global networks of prayer.** Peter and Doris Wagner,[4] co-ordinators for the AD2000 and Beyond Movement Prayer Track, have links with dozens of prayer networks around the world–with millions of Christians involved–**The Day to Change the World** (now becoming an annual event on a day in October involving millions to pray for the nations, Gateway cities, Key Unreached Peoples), **The Marches for Jesus** (involving 16 million by 1995 with a major component of praying for world evangelization), **Intercessors International** (launched by Dennis Clark in 1969), **Concerts of Prayer International** (in which God has used David Bryant to revive the vision of the great Jonathan Edwards two centuries ago), **The Lydia Fellowship** (mobilizing women for intercession), **The Esther Network** (mobilizing children as intercessors), The YWAM initiative to mobilize Christians to fast and pray for the Muslim World during Ramadan and many more.

5. **The specific nature of the praying.** A decade ago we were wondering whether most of the unevangelized world would be closing to any form of Christian presence. Yet in answer to prayer, country after country has opened up for witness whether overtly or covertly. Such countries as Nepal, Cambodia, China, Russia, Uzbekistan, Kyrgyzstan, Bulgaria, Ethiopia, and many others are evidence of this. Many of the closing or closed doors have proved to be revolving doors in answer to prayer.

We are, therefore, in the early stages of a prayer–fueled advance of the Kingdom of Christ–a fact that gives me great

---

[4] The bibliography at the end of this section does not do justice to the prolific productivity of books authored by the Wagners - please refer to the bibliographies of the earlier two sections.

hope for the future despite the evident negatives in the world and failures of the Church. What could happen for the Kingdom if that prayer mobilization further increased? The majority of evangelical churches have yet to catch this vision, the wider world is so big, complex and remote and their own outreach often discouraging. Their energies and resources are spent on local concerns and programs that benefit the gathered saints more than the millions of Satan's captives heading for a lost eternity.

2. *The Biblical Basis*

a. The Promises of Scripture

So many and powerful are the references to the power and importance of prayer that we sin if we fail to pray to our heavenly Father interceding for a lost world, a needy Church, a limping army of the Lord's servants (1 Sam 12:23, 1 Thess 5:17). Yet how weak, short, limited, selfish our prayers so often are. We have a Father who delights to receive us in His Throne room, not only to hear our hesitant requests, but to answer above all that we could ask or expect (Jer 33:3).

Hans von Staden, the Founder and Director of the Dorothea Mission in South Africa, was a mighty man of prayer. He was an inspiration to those of us whom he led. In fact, it was his vision for taking up the challenge given by Andrew Murray for weeks of prayer for the world (Murray 1900:167ff) that led to his request to write the very first **Operation World**. It was he who also suggested the title. He had some pithy comments; several being:

The miracle would be that God NOT answer prayer. He has so committed Himself to answer that it is no miracle that we receive an answer!

When man works, man works; when man prays, God works.

We should not pray for our ministry; prayer is our ministry.

I see so many clear promises about prayer and the assurance of answers in Scripture. How can I even select several and do justice to them? Psalm 2 always impresses me. Here is the spiritual warfare vividly portrayed as the Son meditates on the futility of the opposition and assurance of total victory. The Son repeats the promise given to Him:

> Ask of Me and I will make the nations your heritage, and the ends of the earth your possession. You shall break them with a rod of iron, (Ps 2:8-9 RSV).

Here is the plea of the Father that the Son pray and specifically ask the Father for the world. This Jesus did in His earthly life. Prayer was fundamental to His ministry of redemption for the world. It should be in our ministry too. Amazingly in Rev 2:26 we see Ps 2:9 applied to believers as well. We too are charged by our Father to ask for and rule over the nations as a kingdom of priests.

Do we really grasp the significance of the atonement—how the Triune God identified with us sinful men in the incarnation so that through the Cross we, who are redeemed by faith through grace, are joined to Christ. We are a kingdom of priests identified with His death, resurrection, ascension and present reign (1 Pet 2:9; Rev 1:4-7; 5:10; Rom 5:17). We are now identified with God Himself, seated with Christ in heavenly places sharing in all that He is and has (Col 3:1-4). The greatest of all these is sharing with Him in the ministry of intercession.

It is an awesome thing that we are all called into such a ministry of intercession. We become co-workers with God (1 Cor 3:9, Is 64:4, Mk 16:20). Prayer is the only human activity that moves heaven (Rev 5:9, 8:4-5). In fact in his deep booklet, **With Christ in the School of Prayer**, Andrew Murray shows how our prayers enter into eternity and work together with God in the extension of His Kingdom and even in the formulation of His eternal decrees. I do not pretend to understand this, but I do know that prayer is not a manipulative tool for us to force a reluctant God to do what we want. Nor is it a means for God to gain entrance into our being to manipulate us. I pray not just because I need to obey God, but because He has so ordained that

this is the means by which He will work in this world.   Note
Murray's words (Italics mine):

> This perfect, harmonious union of Divine sover-
> eignty and human liberty is an unfathomable
> mystery because God as **the Eternal One** tran-
> scends all our thoughts. But let it be our comfort
> and strength to know that in the eternal fellow-
> ship of the Father and the Son, the power of
> prayer has its origin and certainty. *Through our*
> *union with the Son, our prayer is taken up and*
> *can have its influence in the inner life of the*
> *Blessed trinity.* God's decrees are no iron frame-
> work against which man's liberty struggles
> vainly. God Himself is living love, Who in His
> Son as man has entered into the tenderest rela-
> tionship with all that is human. Through the
> Holy Spirit, He takes up everything human into
> the Divine life of love, leaving Himself free *to give*
> *every human prayer its place in the government of*
> *the world* (Murray 1900:128ff).

b. The Challenges of the Lord Jesus

The numerous promises, extensive teaching and prayer-
ful life of the Lord Jesus all show the importance of intercession.
Here is not the place to expand on this, but just to share one extraordinary passage where Jesus taught His disciples about
prayer. I refer to John 14:12-14 (RSV):

> Truly, truly, I say to you, he who believes in Me
> will also do the works that I do; and greater
> works than these will he do, because I go to the
> Father. Whatever you ask in My name I will do
> it, that the Father may be glorified in the Son; if
> you ask anything in My name, I will do it.

What are the greater works? Many times I have asked
Christians to explain the meaning, but rarely have I heard what
I believe to be the answer. Some have suggested working mira-
cles, raising the dead, winning multitudes, casting out demons,

more conversions, but these are all works that Jesus did in abundance and promised that we will also do. That still leaves the question, what are the greater works? I believe that this is intercession in the name of the conquering, risen, reigning Lord Jesus Christ. This challenge is followed by a promise that is deliberately repeated for emphasis about asking in prayer and the assurance that Jesus will do it. That is an awesome promise for spiritual warfare and for world evangelization.

The world is going to be evangelized only through prayer. This is the ultimate weapon, the master strategy for overthrowing every plan, argument, power structure, bondage and even the gates of Hades that are in opposition to the King of kings and Lord of lords. Through the Cross He conquered, through applying the victory of the Cross we become more than conquerors. We don't have to understand its efficacy, we just believe the promises of God in the Bible. I have been moved by the ready acceptance of simple African believers that if they pray for someone to be delivered they expect it to happen. May we return to the profound simplicity of trust in a Father who, if we ask, will give (Luke 11:9 - 13).

Intercessory prayer is the means by which we exercise the authority of Christ in the world. There is a power in prayer that takes it outside of time and place. It is perhaps important to emphasize that prayer's power is not diminished by passage of time. God knows how to store up prayer for answers to be revealed much later. Nor is prayer limited by distance. Prayers in one continent immediately have an impact on the situation in another. Prayer walks are now becoming a big emphasis as a missions strategy.[5] It is important to realize that the physical presence of the intercessor does not increase the power of the prayers–though the insights gained, the time set aside for the walk, the commitment involved and the combined, earnest agreement of the participants are all ingredients in the strengthening of faith and the effectiveness of the intercession. Prayer

---

[5] The theology of prayerwalking needs to be spelled out. There is a danger that if the premise of territorial spirits is accepted, this can easily extend to the premise that physical presence of intercessors in the area controlled by the territorial spirit is essential for its binding. The practice of prayer walking needs to be examined - I see many negatives; the huge expense to the detriment of funding for workers on the front line, the motivations for going can be mixed, the drain on the time and energies of workers serving in glamorous places. It can even endanger ministries in sensitive areas.

moves the Hand that moves the universe. So it is being in His presence, rather than in a physical location, that pulls down strongholds.

3. The Personal Challenge

Our effectiveness in spiritual warfare is not dependent on technique or intimate knowledge of the situation, but rather on our relationship to God. Only as I know who I am as a believer and know the revealed will of God for me will I be able to confidently exercise the authority delegated to me. Ignorance of these opens me up to all the wiles and deceptions of the enemy. Tragically, we no longer emphasize these basics. Here are, briefly, what I regard as some of the most important.

a. To Know Our Position in Christ

Redemption in Him

How little is preached on the precious blood of Jesus, the meaning of repentance from dead works and faith in the finished work of Christ on the Cross! What a privilege, what security to be IN Christ–the message of Ephesians. I am redeemed; I now belong to Jesus. I am in the hand of both Jesus and the Father (John 10:27-30). No one can pluck me from that double clasp. Greater is He that is in me than he who is in the world (1 John 4:4). The only danger is my sin which gives Satan his opportunity. Lack of understanding of these basics, results in too many Christians being "poorly born." Jill, my late wife, often used to say, "It seems that to be a Christian today you need to give your heart to Jesus and have 50 years of counselling!" There is a counselling craze that has swept through modern Christianity which has become almost a substitute for the objective truths of redemption in Christ. I am not against biblical counselling, but so much that is termed such is a masquerade using biblical verses which overlay humanistic premises and modern psychology. It leads to a dependence on counsellors and not on God alone and is far from the truth recovered in the Reformation–the priesthood of all believers.

I cannot be affected by witchcraft when walking with God. Stephen Lungu,[6] a long-time colleague and close friend in Zimbabwe, often used to stand in our big evangelistic tent and boldly say, "I am staying at the house over there; you can try to practice your witchcraft on me but it won't work because I belong to Jesus." That in an African context was a tremendous testimony. Many Christians live in fear that they or their loved ones may have inadvertently been exposed to some form of witchcraft or the occult. Missionary friends of ours once traveled back by ship to their homeland for furlough. For years afterwards they were troubled because they blamed subsequent problems with one of their sons on the fact that there was an occultist in the adjoining cabin during the voyage. We can rest assured that no attack of the devil can touch us (1 John 5:18-19) so long as we obey the conditions for abiding in Christ.

I cannot be harmed by curses when walking in obedience to God. In 1990 Jill and I had to go to the house of a friend who had been tricked out of much of her capital and was even being deprived of her house by a con man who had been given hospitality. He had once been a Baptist pastor and manipulated our friend through purported prophecies and speaking in tongues. We had to take strong action to have him evicted from the house and as we left the house he cursed us. Our friend was convinced that the cancer diagnosed in Jill a few months later was the result of that curse. It was with some difficulty we persuaded her that we were immune to such in Jesus (Gen 27:29; Prov 26:2), and that He had all under His control[7] and had encouraged us with specific words from Scripture on this. In fact, in retrospect, we realized that the early symptoms of the cancer had been there before the cursing incident. We were sure of our security in Christ, so these words did not rock our equilibrium, but how easily it could have done so (Rom 8:38-39). In the 1970s we had a strange incident at our Dorothea Mission Bible School in Harare, Zimbabwe. A gardener employed on the grounds was sacked, but on the side he was a practicing witchdoctor. He placed a curse on our people and the property in retaliation. At

---

[6] Stephen Lungu was for many years an evangelist with the Dorothea Mission. He is now one of the leaders in African Enterprise based in Malawi, but with a global ministry. His life story has been published under the title Freedom Fighter by Anne Coombes, 1994, Kingsway, England.

7 Jill lived to complete her book **You Can Change the World** just before she went to be with Jesus in June 1992.

that time two of the ladies were involved in a bitter war of words and this gave the occasion the enemy needed. There were many unpleasant incidents that were only explicable by the demonic. One of the students (now a respected leader of a significant ministry in Zimbabwe) had the experience in a dormitory with other students in the room of being roused screaming in pain because he had been burnt by a hot hand under his blanket at night—the burn marks of the hand were evident in the morning. It was only after the fellowship breakdown was dealt with in repentance and prayer made to drive out these demonic forces that these incidents ceased.

Deliverance in Him

I am free (John 8:36); in Christ I am a new creation (2 Cor 5:17). The Fall in the Garden caused my spiritual death. It affected my spirit and thereby tainted and warped my God–given personality. New birth and life in the Spirit gave me a new start, but sanctification changes my attitudes and actions so that all may be under the lordship of Christ and dependent on Him. My personality created by God is now free to be what God had originally intended when He created it. It is sad that the word "flesh" in the older translations of the Bible has been so misunderstood. The best, though not necessarily all-inclusive, definition I know is in the long and brilliant coverage of the subject by Watchman Nee in **The Spiritual Man** (Nee 1968:69ff). The flesh is any attitude or action done without total dependence on the Lord Jesus Christ (Rom 7:25; 14:23). The NIV has further muddied the theological waters by frequently translating the Greek "sarx" as "sinful nature." Fallen human nature is not a biblical term but frequently used and gives the impression that I have a fallen personality. Knowing my new creaturehood in Jesus is the great liberation from all my genealogical, social, sinful past. Repentance, renunciation of the works of darkness in my own life and in my heredity, and faith in the efficacy of the blood of Christ, sets me free. His indwelling life is my life and I am free to be the person God originally made me to be.

As I look back to my years in Africa working among a people among whom the practice and fear of witchcraft was normal, I am surprised how few of those who were soundly converted needed deliverance ministry—some did, and demons had to be expelled in the name of Jesus. We made a point of ensuring that any seeker faced up to the total commitment needed, which also involved the destruction of all occult charms and medicines and open testimony to family and peers.[8] A solid conversion cleared up many of the problems of association with the powers of darkness.

There was a time at our mission headquarters in Britain when deliverance ministry became a major issue and many sought help. One missionary of another agency staying with us for a course had deep spiritual problems. She approached Jill saying that she believed Jill could help her. Jill told her that if she wanted deliverance ministry she ought to go to others, but if she was willing, Jill would spend half an hour with her and show her who she was in Christ and that she could be different for the rest of her life. This lady was a prime candidate for deliverance—depressed, an alcoholic father and an identical twin sister who was seeking to use the occult on her. However she saw by faith the secret of her new—creaturehood and was free from then on. Months later she wrote thankfully to tell us that she was indeed changed! Too often people run around looking for dramatic spiritual deliverances when a good dose of humility in repentance and renunciation is what is needed.

Seated with Him

I have often heard people say, "When you have troubles you should look up (to the Lord)." I respond that we ought to do the opposite—when we have troubles we look down! Do we realize what Jesus has done for us? Not only are we dead, buried and raised with Him to new life (Rom 6:1-11), but we are also ascended with Him in heavenly places to share now in His reign and throne (Eph 2:6) and this is where our real life is hidden (Col 3:1-4). We are with Christ in the control room of the universe. Do we realize this; do we live in the reality of this? It will revolutionize our prayer life if we embrace this truth. My intercession makes a difference. We are a holy priesthood standing be-

---

[8] The Scriptural pattern is to destroy all occultic articles (Acts 19:18-19). For that reason I would advise all Christians to avoid keeping such articles even for deputation programs. Whatever one's view of the attachment of demons to inanimate objects, there are dangers-whether moral (causing others or ourselves to stumble) or spiritual (demonic influence). It certainly can miscommunicate!

tween God and man with one foot on earth and the other in the
heavenlies. With one ear we hear what is going on down below
and with the other we hear what God is saying. What privileges
we have in Him.

b. To Know the Will of God

Guidance is the birthright of a child of God (Rom 8:14).
Jesus promised us as His friends that we would know, as He did,
what the Father says and does (John 15:14-15). He promised
that the coming of the Holy Spirit would both teach and remind
us what Jesus spoke, but would also guide us into all the truth
(John 14, 16)–both the written Word and in our day to day walk
with Jesus. All Bible-believing Christians agree with the former.
It is the latter which is open to discussion and abuse, yet is essential for effectiveness in prayer and in spiritual warfare. If I
know that I am where God placed me and doing what He has
shown me, no suffering, no attacks of the enemy will deflect me
until I gain the assurance that it is my Father's will for a change.
Many a missionary in a hard field has been kept true to God's
calling because of that conviction that God personally revealed
His will. All over the world I have challenged Christian workers
with these words, "Never leave for negative reasons where God
has placed you." The enemy of souls will do all he can to provide
all possible negatives and convince us that this is God's guidance. Over the years I have been moved at how many have come
back, often years later, and said that that particular word I had
spoken kept them in God's will.

In day-to-day ministry the Holy Spirit uses many ways to
prompt God's servants–the Word or a particular verse that comes
to us in deep power as His Word to me, other people, circumstances, or most frequently the deep inner conviction or burden
to pray, speak or take some action. We have the mind of Christ
(1 Cor 2:16), so there is often that deep inner knowing that comes
from the Spirit which is hard to explain. All of these promptings
are subservient to the absolute of Scripture and have to be held
loosely and in humility. We can sometimes get it wrong. Yet
how often that gift of the Spirit of a word of knowledge, wisdom
or prophecy has been spoken into situations in a redemptive way!
This has to be self-authenticating–the witness of the Spirit in
others too. It is very hard to give any corrective advice to one
who says "The Lord has guided me," or "Thus says the Lord."

I have not the time nor space to share wonderful accounts of God's guidance in this way, but how we need that leading in intercession. I share but one from my own life. For many years I have kept a special prayer list specifically for prayer burdens I believe the Lord assigned to me for intercession. It is astonishing to look back on what must now be over 500 definite prayer requests—only about 40 of which are still active. Nearly all the rest have been answered—with some I had the deep conviction that God had already answered before I saw the answer, but most were crossed off when I saw the answer. We cannot intercede for everything. We need that leading of the Spirit to those that are our corporate or individual responsibility. We have a God who speaks today, who communicates with us so that we exercise a ministry through revelation. What liberation to know that my Father will always show me what to pray for, which sick person should receive healing, what to preach, where to go, how to write a letter, as well as discern the wiles of the enemy.

There are terms rarely heard today: "effectual praying" and "praying through." Elijah was one who prayed this way (Jas 5:16-17). As Elijah prayed on Carmel for rain he knew that God would answer, even though he had to send his servant seven times before the cloud became visible. The New Testament is even more explicit on this way of praying:

> And this is the confidence which we have in him, that if we ask anything according to His will He hears us. And if we know that He hears us in whatever we ask, we know that we HAVE obtained the requests made of Him. 1 John 5:14-15.

Jesus said:

> I say to you, if you have faith as a grain of mustard seed, you will say to this mountain,'Move from here to there' and it will move; and nothing will be impossible to you. Matt 17:20.

We need to know far more about this depth of prayer in today's battle as we come into the final supreme effort to evangelize the world. We need to know the mind of God (1 John 5:14), be agreed together (Matt 18:19-20) and know that what we ask in the name of Jesus will be granted. We can then say the word of faith to the situation knowing that we have the answer. We can then praise expecting to see the deliverance. The battle is usually more severe than these words may sound, but the principles are there. So it was in the prayer lives of great men of God such as Andrew Murray of South Africa, George Müller of Bristol, Rees Howells of Wales, Praying Hyde of Pakistan. In our own mission agency, WEC International, Norman Grubb (the biographer of Rees Howells) brought us into these basic principles for the growth and advance of our work (Grubb 1940).

I use one illustration from recent years. In 1990 we held our sixth annual International Leaders Conference in Scotland. During one of our many prayer sessions, our leaders from Senegal in West Africa shared their concern. Senegal is over 90% Muslim and was to host the World Islamic Conference in their capital the following year. The leaders of the Muslim nations were to gather to discuss united action on a number of fronts, one being the ending of all Christian mission work and the elimination of indigenous Christian minorities in their lands. After prayer, we shared together how we believed God was leading us as to what to ask. We all agreed that we must pray for the nullification of the impact of that conference. We had a mighty time of prayer which reached a climax when a deep conviction came that God had heard and we ended with glorious praise. The Gulf War came a few months later. This event so polarized the Muslim world that the conference was postponed. When at last the conference was convened the following year the divisions were still so marked that most of the leaders left the conference before the scheduled time with little decided. God stepped in to thwart the plottings of the rulers of this world (Ps 2:1-3) in answer to those definite prayers in which we were sure of God's answer long before the event.

c. To Use the Weapons God has Provided

We have no need to fear anything the devil can do. We respect his power and understand that detached from the Lord Jesus we are fair game for him. God has given all we need to both defend ourselves and also to take the offensive in the warfare against Satan's wiles, principalities, powers and world rulers of this present darkness. Here I can only refer to two important passages as illustration of this truth.

Ephesians 6 is beloved by all Christians because of the superb description Paul gives of our spiritual armor. He shows each part of the soldier's armor has deep spiritual application to our total defense for life in a non-Christian world permeated by sin and also every stratagem and attack of Satan. He also shows us the mighty weapons for attack—the sword of the Spirit, the Word of God, and prayer in the Spirit. The strong message is that we need to be constantly in close fellowship with our God, or we are in danger of ineffectiveness in ministry, or worse become a victim of Satan's wiles or fiery darts. There have been too many examples of servants of God who have become deeply immersed in the area of spiritual warfare, but have failed to put on and maintain that armor daily and have become casualties themselves.

Revelation 12 is an amazing chapter. I believe it is a key chapter in a book written as a manual for spiritual warfare. There are many interpretations of the symbolisms in this chapter into which I do not go here, but I believe this chapter gives a picture of the warfare of Satan against the Seed of the woman (the Lord Jesus Christ) and the woman (the people of God throughout history from the Garden to the Consummation). In this amazing chapter, the Holy Spirit exposes Satan and his weapons. Nowhere else in Scripture are we told so many of Satan's names, functions and titles. He is revealed in his true colors as never before. He is the accuser of the brethren, the deceiver of the whole world and, by implication, the one who engineers compromise among believers. Yet here we are also shown the three invincible weapons God has given us:

1. For Satan's weapon of accusation we have the Blood of the Lamb. My safety is not in knowledge of the enemy's stratagems and the precautions I take, but in the efficacy of the blood of the Lamb once slain to deal with the sin issue—Satan has no more claim on me once I have repented and continue to walk in the light. I have total freedom and life more abundant whatever my suffering, difficulties or stress in the battle. I am totally safe in Jesus.

2. For Satan's weapon of deceit we have the word of testimony. This testimony is first about who Christ is and what He has done. Then I can boldly say what God has made me in Christ, what God promises me in His Word, what I know my prayers can achieve and what the ultimate conclusion of the war will be. I have the witness of the Holy Spirit who assures me of

these things. He gives me the words to utter whatever my circumstances. He gives assurance that God can use even me to testify so that the devil's captives have their blindness removed and can be set free. The Holy Spirit also gives discernment in every situation. We can have that gift of inner knowing what is of God and what is of Satan; His peace being our referee whistle-blower. This testimony becomes the means by which those enslaved to the prince of this world through their belief systems, practices, moral actions and spiritual bondages are liberated.

3. For Satan's weapon of compromise we have to be totally committed. We love not our lives even unto death. That is the extent to which we are willing to go for Jesus sake. Over such the enemy has no hold. How we need to walk in that total abandonment to God. Any compromise lays us open to the enemy. The more dangerous we are to his kingdom the greater our humility, dependence and commitment to our Lord must be.

d. To Exercise Our Delegated Authority

The Great Commission as expressed by Jesus in Matthew 28:18-20 shows that through the victory of the Cross all authority in heaven and on earth have been given to Him. In Christ we have been delegated His authority (Luke 9:1; 10:19). Jesus has given us the keys of the Kingdom (Matt 16:19). By faith we can move mountains. We have the power to bind and loose (Matt 18:18-19, Jn 20:23). This gives us the boldness to take kingdoms (Dan 7:14, 22, 27), expect miracles, command demons to submit to our word of command in the name of Jesus, break down strongholds (2 Cor10:4), resist and bind Satan (1 Pet 5:9), spoil the strong man's goods and bring release to his captives in the name of Jesus. All we can say is to repeat Paul's triumphant words, "If God is for us who can be against us." They don't have a chance!

The victory of the Lord Jesus in His cross and resurrection over sin, death and Satan was so decisive that we only have to apply that victory to any opposition of the enemy. I cannot agree with the title of Hal Lindsay's book, **Satan is alive and well** on Planet Earth. Satan has been mortally wounded, his defeat irreversible. He is not well (Rev 12:10-12)! Simple believers in Africa, Asia and Latin America expect God to work in these ways. We Western Christians make things so theological

and complicated. If God says it, of course He will do it! All His
enemies are now being put under His feet (Heb 10:14) and we by
faith ensure the continuation of the process (Luke 10:17-19).
What confidence this gives, what assurance that as we walk with
the Lord in the center of His will every assault on us will ultimately fail, and every advance we make will ultimately bear
fruit for eternity.

Too often believers have the impression that they have to
go out and do the fighting, not seeing that the battle is the
Lord's. I have seen deliverance sessions where those praying
seem to think spiritual authority is measurable by vocal volume
or physical activity. It also troubles me that many in their
praying can be presumptuous and demand or claim things beyond our sphere of authority. Note how Jude writes in warning
that we be humble in this area:

> But when the archangel Michael, contending
> with the devil, disputed about the body of Moses,
> he did not presume to pronounce a reviling judg-
> ment upon him, but said, "The Lord rebuke you."
> But these men revile whatever they do not un-
> derstand (Jude 9-10).

An over-emphasis on deliverance ministry can be un-
healthy and even dangerous. There is a place for it, but this
course should be pursued when it is plain that demonization is
the issue. Arthur Neil, a Baptist pastor used of God in the life of
a witch, Doreen Irvine, has written two masterly and biblical
volumes dealing with this whole area (Neil 1990, 1991; Irvine,
1973). He shared with me that in all his long experience in
ministering in the area of deliverance from demonic activity, he
only has had to deal with two clear cases of demon possession
but many more with oppressions and attacks of various kinds—
the latter being the more difficult to deal with. Jill and I had to
make an urgent pastoral visit to one of our Latin American
fields.   One of the problems we faced concerned an over-
involvement with deliverance ministry. One of our most effective church planting missionaries had become so involved with
delivering Christians from demons. She claimed that thousands
of demons had to be cast out of pastors in her many months of
ministry around the country. This ministry was causing dismay

to many, and appeared to be even possibly a side-tracking of the enemy into endless conversations with demons and time-consuming deliverances. She was even cross-examining lesser demons to find out more concerning the upper echelons of the demonic hierarchy. We sought to warn her of the real dangers associated with the latter and the need for a rounded balance in ministry in the former. I cannot help but feel that she was lay-ing herself open to believing the lies and distortions of the enemy and having all her energies consumed in this deliverance minis-try. She took some of our advice and moderated some of the ex-cesses in her ministry.

How we need a holy caution in this area. We do not seek the demonic in everything, but we deal with any evident mani-festation of demonic powers. Doreen Irvine with her background of Satanism and witchcraft followed by years of ministry and counselling wrote these words:

> There was no long dialogue with the demon.
> There is no need for that. Jesus cast out demons
> with one word, 'Go,' and the demons left at once.
> We can cast out demons with six words today: 'Go
> in the name of Jesus'. If demon-possessed people
> are willing to be free and are repentant of their
> sins, demons have to go at once. The devil is
> highly delighted with eight hour deliverance
> meetings, which last until three in the morning,
> while demons play hide and seek , wear out
> Christians, confound them with their knowledge,
> and frighten them by their strength (Irvine
> 1986:129).

e. To Pay the Price of Being an Intercessor

I cannot conclude without a word of caution. There is always a price to pay. Grace was freely given to us in Christ, and is freely available to us day by day. But if we are to become ministers of that grace it will cost. We therefore rejoice in our sufferings for the sake of others and in our flesh we complete what is lacking in Christ's afflictions for the sake of His body (Col 1:24). There are the death points in every ministry to deal with our self-reliance (2 Cor 1:8-11). We need to identify totally with the objects of our intercession as did Moses (Exod 32:32),

Paul (Rom 9:3), and also the Lord Jesus Christ Himself (Is 53:12). This was true of Elisha's intercession for the son of the Shunammite woman. Gehazi's use of Elisha's staff did nothing for the boy; it needed costly and committed intercession for the boy to be raised up (2 Ki 18-37). There is the danger in spiritual warfare that we rely on the staffs of techniques and experience and not on the total costly commitment for true and eternal deliverances.

Conclusion

Never before has the completion of world evangelization been such a possibility as in our present generation! The basic minimum requirements given by the Lord Jesus Christ in the Great Commission in its various renderings could be attainable in our generation. In Mark 16 we are commanded to preach the Gospel to every person. And in Matthew 28:18-20 to make disciples of every ethnic people (the Greek meaning for the word "nation" most frequently used in English translations). My estimation is that 15%-20% of the world's population is beyond the present preaching of the Gospel. Of the 12,000 peoples in the countries of the world, an estimated 2,000-2,500 have yet to see a missiological breakthrough to produce a viable church-planting movement within the culture. Possibly only 1,000 or so have very little being done on a long-term basis to ensure their evangelization.

The task is achievable, but at a cost. The major commitment must be to intercession so that every barrier—whether moral, political or spiritual—be broken down and the Kingdom of the Lord Jesus Christ come. Let us not allow anything to deflect us from the real goal which is world evangelization and a new heaven and a new earth where righteousness dwells and all evil is forever banished!

References Cited

Dawson, John
    1989   *Taking our Cities for God.* Word Publishing,
            Word UK Ltd, Milton Keynes, England.
Duewel, Wesley
    1986   *Touch the World Through Prayer.* Marshall
            Pickering, Basingstoke, Hants, England.
Garnett, Mary
    1979   *Take your Glory, Lord; William Duma's Life
            Story.* Baptist Publishing house,
            Roodepoort,South Africa.
Grubb, Norman G.
    1940   *Touching the Invisible.* Lutterworth Press,
            London, England.
    1952   *Rees Howells, Intercessor.* Lutterworth Press,
            London, England.
Irvine, Doreen
    1973   *From Witchcraft to Christ.* Concordia Publishing,
            England.
    1986   *Spiritual Warfare.* Marshall Pickering,
            Basingstoke, Hants, England.
Jacobs, Donald R.
    1990   Out of Africa: Evangelism and Spiritual Warfare.
    In *Wrestling with Dark Angels.* (Ed. by C. Peter Wag-
    ner and F. Douglas Pennpyer). Ventura, CA: Regal
    Books, pp 303-312.
Johnstone, Jill K.
    1993   *You Can Change the World.* OM Publishing,
            Carlisle, Cumbria, England.
Johnstone, Patrick J.
    1974   *Operation World - Edition 1.* Dorothea Mission,
            Pretoria, South Africa.
    1993   *Operation World - Edition 5.* OM Publishing,
            Carlisle, Cumbria, England.
Latourette, Kenneth Scott
    1970   *A History of the Expansion of Christianity.*
            Zondervan, Grand Rapids, Michigan, USA.

Murray, Andrew
>   1900   *The Key to the Missionary Problem.* Christian Literature Crusade.
>   1981   *With Christ in the School of Prayer.* Whitaker House, Springdale, PA, USA.

Nee, Watchman
>   1968   *The Spiritual Man - Vol. 1.* Christian Fellowship Publishers, Inc., New York, USA.

Neil, Arthur
>   1989   *Aid Us in Our Strife, Vol. 1.* Heath Christian Trust, England.
>   1990   *Aid Us in Our Strife, Vol. 2.* Nova Publishing Ltd., Newton Abbot, Devon, England.

Penn-Lewis, Jessie
>   1912   *War on the Saints.* Overcomer Literature Trust.

Peretti, Frank
>   1986   *This Present Darkness.* Good News Publishers, Westchester, IL, USA.
>   1989   *Piercing the Darkness.* Crossway Books, Westchester, IL, USA.

Pierson, Arthur T.
>   1899   *George Müller of Bristol.* Fleming H. Revell Co., Westwood, NJ, USA.

Sangster, Thelma
>   1984   *The Torn Veil.* Marshalls, England.

Taylor, Mr. and Mrs. Howard
>   1918   *Hudson Taylor and the China Inland Mission.* CIM, England.

Tucker, Ruth
>   1983   *From Jerusalem to Irian Jaya.* Zondervan, Grand Rapids, Michigan, USA.

Wagner, Peter
>   1990   *Wrestling with Dark Angels.* Regal Books, Venture, CA, USA.

Wakeley, Mike
>   1995   A Critical Look at a New "Key" to Evangelization. *Evangelical Missions Quarterly* 31(2): 152-162 .